Advance Praise For
On The Wing of Eternity

"In this beautifully written book about the life and death of a young pilot who flew with Britain's RAF in World War II, Michael Alexander has crafted a love letter to the father he never knew. Decades after James Alexander was killed in a bombing raid over Rotterdam, his son began excavating his father's life. The result is a poignant, at times heartbreaking portrait of a sensitive, gifted young man, deeply in love with his wife and baby son, but who in the end sacrificed it all for the cause of freedom."

—LYNNE OLSON, author of *Those Angry Days* and *Citizens of London*

"The words 'Life, Love and War' sum up the story of Canadian Jimmy Alexander, who joined the RAF, followed to England by his fiancée Bar, who defied the U-Boat hazards of the Atlantic, to marry and give birth to the author. Compiled from journals and family memories, and written in the first person, this book is bloody good – read it!"

—LIEUTENANT COLONEL IAN BLACKWELL, former Lecturer, Royal Military Academy, Sandhurst, UK, author of *Fifth Army in Italy 1943-1945*

"Through flashbacks and recollections, Jimmy Alexander shares with us, highlights from his youth, his training as a pilot in the RAF, the terror of enemy raids, and the bittersweet bonds forged with his crew and other airmen. As his missions grow more perilous and losses mount, we hold onto hope that he will survive. Author Michael Alexander made the bold choice to tell the story in his father's voice - with all of the honesty and emotion that filled Jimmy's journals and letters to his family - and the story is richer for it. This is a gripping tale of love, courage, camaraderie and coming of age. It is a haunting tribute to those who serve and a powerful meditation on the cost and significance of duty."

—CANDICE SHY HOOPER, author of *Delivered Under Fire: Absalom Markland and Freedom's Mail*

"Flying into combat requires an acceptance of immense risk. Eighty-five years ago, this was particularly true. With limited technology, and few safety protocols, pilots like Jimmy Alexander faced great peril every time they took to the skies. It's difficult to fathom the toll it must have taken, flying bombing missions day after day during World War II; but this book captures it brilliantly. The courage and dedication of those young men are an inspiration to those flying combat missions today."

—LIEUTENANT COLONEL JUSTIN MORELAND, Combat Mission Ready F-35 Pilot, United States Air Force

On The Wing *of* Eternity

On The Wing *of* Eternity

Memory of Life, Love and War

Michael O. Alexander

CASPER PRESS

Casper Press, June 2025

Copyright @ 2025 by Michael O. Alexander
All rights reserved.

Published in the United States by Casper Press,
Boca Grande, FL
A Division of The International Forum, Inc.

Alexander, Michael O.
On The Wing of Eternity: Memory of Life,
Love and War / by Michael O. Alexander –
Boca Grande, FL : Casper Press, 2025.
264 pages, 2.22 cm
Includes bibliographic references
ISBN (Hardcover) 978-0-9973203-6-7
ISBN (Paperback) 978-0-9973203-7-4
Library of Congress Control Number: 2025935681
BISAC 1. HISTORY / Wars & Conflicts / World War II / General
2. HISTORY / Wars & Conflicts / World War II / European Theater
3. HISTORY / Canada / General
4. BIOGRAPHY & AUTOBIOGRAPHY / Military
5. HISTORY / Europe / Great Britain / 20th Century

Book design by Sally Stetson Design

2 4 6 8 10 9 7 5 3

*For the men and women who risk their lives
to protect our country and defend our freedom*

Courage is the price that Life extracts for granting peace.
The soul that knows it not, knows no release from little things:
Knows not the livid loneliness of fear,
Nor mountain heights where bitter joy can hear
The sound of wings.

AMELIA EARHART

CONTENTS

FOREWORD

August 28, 1941, 07:00, *Attlebridge Airfield, Norfolk, England* 1

PART ONE : *Life and Love*

CHAPTER 1	**Taking Off**	7
CHAPTER 2	**First Landing**	19
CHAPTER 3	**Family**	27
CHAPTER 4	**School Years**	35
CHAPTER 5	**Summers**	59
CHAPTER 6	**Military College**	75
CHAPTER 7	**Learning to Fly**	105

PART TWO : *Love and War*

CHAPTER 8 **Off to War,** *April 1940* 121

CHAPTER 9 **London,** *May 1940* 133

CHAPTER 10 **France,** *June 1940* 143

CHAPTER 11 **England,** *Summer 1940* 151

CHAPTER 12 **Iceland,** *September 1940* 159

CHAPTER 13 **Northern Ireland,** *November 1940* 173

CHAPTER 14 **Suffolk,** *December 1940* 179

CHAPTER 15 **Belfast,** *Winter 1941* 183

CHAPTER 16 **England,** *April 1941* 189

CHAPTER 17 **Belfast,** *Spring 1941* 193

CHAPTER 18 **Norfolk,** *Summer 1941* 199

August 28, 1941, 17:39, *Attlebridge Airfield, Norfolk, England*...221

AFTERWORD 223
Family Tree 240
References and Sources 242
Acknowledgments 244
Author Biography 247

FOREWORD

My father was killed when he was 23 and I was less than a year old. During my youth, people often said, "Oh, you were too young to have known him." This was true at the time. But over the years, I came to know him well. His friends and family talked about him often, about his good nature, and sense of humor. I knew he was well-liked.

During the early years of my own life, I followed in my father's footsteps. I attended the same school where, upon the walls of its buildings, I traced his name and his achievements in academics and sports. My bookshelves were, and still are, lined with his leather-bound books on classics and history. They were the prizes he had received for his achievements. As I read each one, I felt his presence, knowing he too had held them in his hands. I wanted so much to be like him. Often, I felt he was there with me, watching me struggle where he had excelled. When I was older, in my thirties, I thought about the life he might have lived. Later still, I wanted to do something to make up for what he missed and for what we missed by not knowing him. I considered telling the story of his life and the fascinating time in which he lived. As his son, I felt I was the best person to do this.

I had plenty of source material: When my mother was still alive, I discovered a dusty old trunk in her basement filled with snapshots of my father's friends, family, school, and summer vacations. I caught glimpses of a youth full of activity and happy times. His chess set, his poetry, and a large box full of silver cups and other prizes reflected his passions and love of sports. When my grandmother passed away, I inherited a large box of his letters and diaries. But it wasn't until my mother died, and I found letters he had sent to her, that I heard his voice. In letters and journals, he described the all-too-familiar struggles of youth: social life, girlfriends, the demands of school and university years, and dreams for the future. Before he decided on military service in Britain's Royal Air Force, he weighed his career choices and discussed them with his parents. Among his papers were letters that he had written during the war to his family and to my mother. He shared his excitement, frustration, and determination as Britain fought for its survival in 1940 and 1941.

My father was born at the end of the First World War. During the two decades of peace and prosperity that followed, a worldwide influenza killed over fifty million people, and the Great Depression cost a quarter of the workforce their jobs. In the aftermath of the Great War, dictators rose to power in Russia, Europe and South America. Communism and Fascism were on the rise, and Germany began rearming under Adolph Hitler.

It was also a time of exciting change and personal liberation. Automobiles gave people more freedom to travel, telephones made the world more connected as they became a standard household fixture, and radio broadcasting brought news and entertainment into the home. Kodak introduced colored film, and air travel began. Hollywood's Golden Era produced movies that both reflected and defined popular culture. With economic growth and social change came an artistic revolution. The 1920s brought the Jazz Age and dance moves like the Charleston and the Turkey Trot. Young women felt liberated and dressed daringly in the flapper style. The older generation saw it all as outrageous and immoral.

An established social structure gave my father and his classmates a code of behavior to follow during this time, one that respected tradition, humility, honesty and a sensitivity to how one's actions affect others. Armed with these values, they matured just in time to fight another war. My father chose a career in the Air Force without ever having flown in an airplane. He could not have guessed at the time of his choice that air combat would become a key to strategic offense and defense in the war.

Like the youth of today, those who grew up in the 1920s and '30s came of age in a dramatically changing and shifting landscape. They worked, had fun, and wondered about their future. But as events unfolded in the 1930s with growing worries about another war, there were questions as to whether governments were adequately prepared. The rise of Nazi Germany and of Japan as threats to a peaceful world was not unlike what free democracies face today, with the same questions of adequate defense and preparation.

In writing this book, I have let my father tell his story. Much of it is in his own words and drawn from his letters and journals. I have also drawn from historical accounts of the times to bring context to his perspective and what he was experiencing. I decided to tell the story from my father's point of view as he sat waiting in the Briefing Room at the airfield in Attlebridge, Norfolk, on August 28, 1941. I have imagined this, of course. Perhaps that day he did take some time to reflect on his short, full life, perhaps he thought about some of the things I have written about here. We will never know. I can only hope he had some sense of his significance before he died.

From the letters and journals, it was clear how devoted my father was to his family, his education and sports. He was also well informed about what was unfolding on the world stage. Part of this came from his father, a General in the Army, who knew what was happening in real time. The two men shared an active correspondence that was interesting to read purely from a modern historical perspective. My father came from a family of service, heavily influenced by the dictates of both church and military. He was also a product of two nations, born in England during the First World War, then growing up in Canada, guided by British tradition. The King was his king, and his flag was the Canadian flag, which was then the Union Jack. Canada was maturing as a nation and proved its importance to the rest of the world throughout the conflict in which my father and his friends would serve.

For my father and his peers, the stakes were clear: Hitler, the Nazi dictator, had to be stopped, or the world would fall under the tyranny of evil. Their lives and the choices they made were guided by their commitment to family, country and each other. Because of their sacrifice, their children and grandchildren have been able to live in peace, and free from tyranny. This is their legacy. It is his legacy.

Michael Alexander
January 2025

An RAF briefing room, 1941.

A Bristol Blenheim IV being prepared for flight by the ground crew at Attlebridge Airfield, 1941.

AUGUST 28, 1941, 07:00
Attlebridge Airfield, Norfolk, England

I was awake before dawn. The bus was already waiting to take us from our billets to the base and the Officers' Mess for the full English breakfast of bacon and eggs. We're gathered now in the Briefing Room with our crews, to learn about today's bombing operations. I can feel the nervous tension of the others as we listen to our orders. The room is a temporary type of building, not large, with a few windows and rows of tables and chairs facing large blackboards and maps on stands. The Wing Commander steps up to tell us about today's raid.

Take-off will be at 14:40. Our target will be the Port of Rotterdam. Our route will take us 140 miles across the North Sea. We will have to fly low over the water to avoid detection as we approach landfall at the Hook of Holland. Our targets are ships, the port, the docks, and factories. And we will be flying between 20 and 50 feet off the ground in daylight.

I have heard that Rotterdam is one of the largest ports occupied by the Germans and is used for much of their intercoastal shipping of supplies. Two weeks ago, a similar raid met with success. There was little defense from enemy ground forces or fighters. Some of our Blenheim aircraft were lost, but most returned safely.

Our briefing continues with reports of the expected weather over the route. The maps of the target are explained in more detail. We hope enemy destroyers and anti-aircraft batteries won't be waiting for us. Our squadrons have been suffering considerable losses in recent weeks. The good news is that 152 Squadron of spitfires will give us fighter escort. That will help keep Luftwaffe's Me109s away from us.

The briefing continues with intelligence on possible enemy defenses and a reminder of what to do if we are shot down or captured. Finally, the Wing Commander gives us the order of flights and engine starting times, and we synchronize our watches. He concludes the briefing by warning, "This time, Jerry might be ready for us."

Now comes the worst part—waiting. I feel butterflies in my stomach. I would love to walk it off. But because of security, we aren't allowed to leave the briefing room. Everyone is quiet, immersed in his thoughts. Some write letters; others look like they are sleeping but they aren't. My stomach is twisting, and I can't seem to calm it down. Fear is something we all deal with. It's a constant companion, but we don't talk about it.

We've just had word that our take-off time has been changed again. We're now expected to depart at 17:20. It's going to be a long day. I had better find something else to think about, something to get my mind off what lies ahead.

PART ONE
Life and Love

Gertrude Williams.   *Ronald Okeden Alexander.*

ONE

TAKING OFF

As far back as I can remember, my life was filled with cousins, aunts and uncles, and grandparents. Of course, I had friends, too, many of them. But it was my family that was my constant guide. They had the greatest influence on me and who I have become.

I was born on June 3, 1918, in Caterham, Surrey, not far from London. The day I was born was my mother's 24th birthday. It was also the King's. At the time, the Great War had been raging for almost four years. My father was in France. He'd been fighting at the Front since 1915. The morning after my birth, the *London Times* was delivered, as it usually was, to the trenches. It contained this brief announcement in its pages:

"R. Both doing very well, G."

It was a message to "R," Ronald, my father, from "G," Gertrude, my mother, announcing my arrival. She knew the *Times* would reach him sooner and more reliably than the mail.

I am a British citizen, as I was born in England. However, because my parents are Canadian, I am also a citizen of Canada. My mother's family came to Canada from England and Wales in the late 18th century and settled in Quebec City.

My father is a more recent immigrant to Canada. At age eighteen, he arrived from England in 1906 to work for the Bank of Montreal and joined the militia and the Royal Canadian Regiment. When war came, he lied about phlebitis in his legs, which would have eliminated him from consideration, and went overseas with the Victoria Rifles and the rank of Major.

His battalion sailed for England in May 1915, and with his horse, he crossed the English Channel by ship to get to the front lines at Hazebrouck, France. During the next four years, he fought in the trenches at Ypres, where he suffered from poisonous gas, and at Mount Sorrell, St. Eloi, the Somme, and Passchendaele. In 1916 and 1917, as Lieutenant Colonel, he became Commanding Officer of the 24th Battalion, Victoria Rifles, and was awarded the Distinguished Service Order (DSO) for his successful command and leadership in action at Courcelette and the Somme.

My father is slim, only 5'6" tall, but fit and always active. His look is penetrating, and though his voice can be commanding, his bark is worse than his bite. When relaxed, he smokes his pipe, plays bridge, and attends to his dogs. He is kind, a good listener, and genuinely interested in your words.

My parents met in Quebec City when my father was stationed there before the war. My mother, Gertrude Williams, was the second daughter of Lennox Williams, then Dean and later Anglican Bishop of Quebec, and his wife, Nan Rhodes. My father once described how they met:

> *I was first invited for Sunday supper at the Williams' home when Gertrude was away in Europe for the year, but I met her older sister, Mary. It wasn't until 1913 that Gertrude and I met casually at parties in Quebec. One evening, we both attended a dinner party, and I did the finest thing I have done. I fell in love with her. Gertrude was 19, and I was 25. I had no money, only three years of service in the regiment, and wouldn't be allowed to marry until I was a captain*

Their courtship was well-established three years later when he went overseas to war, and in January 1916, my mother announced their engagement. A year later, she, her parents, and her sister, Mary, sailed to England. Mary was to be my mother's bridesmaid, but she had also come to see her future husband, Jack Wallace, who was serving with the Canadian Grenadier Guards.

My parents were married in London on February 19, 1917, at Christ Church, Westminster, with my grandfather officiating. At the wedding, "Gertrude followed tradition and wore 'something new and something blue.' It was a blue garter that slipped down her leg as she walked up the aisle."

I was amused whenever my father told this story because I knew my mother would have carried on as though nothing had happened. Such things never put her off, and she would have found it amusing. She has a very good sense of humor.

After the wedding, my father returned to the Front for the rest of the war, except for infrequent and short leaves to visit home. On one very short leave in London, as he and my mother sat down to dinner, he was handed a telegram from his battalion headquarters which read: "Rejoin."

It meant that every soldier on leave had to immediately rejoin their regiment and return to the Front, even if they had just arrived home. At Victoria Station, the scene was heartbreaking. When the train pulled in with those taking leave, a staff officer announced through a megaphone, "All officers arriving from France will cross over the platform and return to the Front." All they could do was speak to their wives over the barrier and go. Many of them would never return.

My mother stayed in England during the war to support my father. It wasn't until six months after I was born that my father saw me for the first time. His leaves from the Front were uncertain and always short, and he and my mother had very little time together. He was able to be at my baptism along with my Alexander grandparents. My paternal grandfather, John Abercromby Alexander, called me "wee Jamie" and carried me from their house to the church. I was given a middle name, Okeden, the same as my father's, and an old English name from my grandmother Alexander's family. For my first name, I was called after my mother's older brother, Lt. James Williams, who was killed in 1916 at the battle of the Somme while serving in the 87th Battalion, Canadian Grenadier Guards. His widow, Evelyn Meredith, was a close friend of my mother's and my Aunt Mary's and had grown up with them in Quebec. She was my Godmother.

After my Christening, my father returned to France, and in October, he participated in the Allies' daily advance into Germany. On November 11, 1918, at 7:26 A.M., a signal was received that read, *"Hostilities will cease at 11:00 hours."*

He would never forget that moment. Every year after, we recognized November 11 as Remembrance Day and wore poppies on our lapels. At eleven o'clock, we stood at attention for a minute of silence. My father told me that the poppies had special significance for him because they grew in the fields near Ypres, where he had fought with his battalion. The poem "In Flanders Fields," written by Dr. John McCrae, a Canadian physician, immortalized the red poppies as a symbol of remembrance.

The casualties of the First World War were enormous. A whole generation of men had died in a conflict that was horrible beyond anyone's imagination. When it ended on November 11, 1918, sixteen million soldiers and civilians had died. As I grew up, adults talked about the war as the event that changed everything. At school, we were told of the courage and sacrifice of those who fought. We learned of the horrors of war, but also examples of human decency, leadership, and care. Canada's losses were 63,018 killed and 149,709 wounded. Seven percent of its population of eight million were in uniform.

I wanted to know more about what the war was really like. My father had kept a diary of what happened to him and his fellow soldiers. This is some of what was in it:

Armies faced each other in their trenches, locked in battle with no winner. The enemy front line trenches were about 100 yards from us. Our lines were protected by barbed wire. The trenches were dry, but as winter weather set in, they deteriorated. The sides crumbled in, and about two feet of water lay on the bottom. Memories of the trenches are mud, and more mud, rats everywhere, the night illuminated by star shells and flares, the putt-putt of machine guns, and the single putt of a bullet.

His diary also describes the poisonous gas attacks:

One night, while sitting in my trench, the whole side was blown out by a shell. One of our chief fears was gas attacks, which were either released from gas cylinders and blown across by the wind or from gas shells. Our gas masks were very primitive. Gas warning gongs were hung everywhere.

The descriptions in his diary were quite vivid about death and destruction, but he also wrote about the good things. On his first Christmas on the battlefields in 1915, he witnessed something rather extraordinary.

Both sides stopped firing. I was in a sniper's spot behind the front line. About noon, I saw a few German heads appear above their parapets, and they waved to us. Our men promptly did the same. In a short time, men from both sides were in no man's land, warily talking to each other and exchanging cigarettes and bully beef. It was an extraordinary sight but fraught with danger. So, as the duty officer, I asked our artillery to fire a few rounds of warning into the enemy's back area. No man's land cleared immediately, but I felt so badly to be spoiling those moments when so many who held similar religious beliefs were sharing the peace of Christmas together.

He also wrote about the strong religious faith of many of his comrades in arms. "I have never known a 'big' soldier who didn't have very strong religious feelings."

When the war began, few thought it would last long, and many signed up to avoid missing it before it was over. No one had expected the awful scale of death and destruction from poisonous gas, machine guns, and continuous barrage from powerful artillery. Britain called on the forces of its Empire – from Canada, Australia, New Zealand, South Africa, India, and others to join the cause. It went badly for both sides, a stalemate at times, with the lines at the front moving back and forth as the Germans and the Allies took turns gaining the advantage. The United States entered the War during the fourth year, in September of 1917, and American troops were not in place until April 1918. They, too, suffered great losses; but America's entry made an important difference to the confidence of the Allied cause. It was a matter of time before Germany reluctantly surrendered.

Growing up in Canada, my friends and I were more interested in our day-to-day lives, but at school we learned about the war in English and history classes. We learned how Britain's Royal Navy had confronted Germany's newly constructed battle fleet and protected supply lines from German U-boat submarines that were doing extensive damage to Allied merchant shipping. Britain's vast empire led the world in trade, and its navy protected this trade by ruling the seas. At the beginning of the war, aircraft were introduced sparingly, mainly for reconnaissance, to discover enemy positions. The Wright brothers had made their first flight only five years before in 1909.

The Royal Air Force (RAF) was established as an independent force at the end of the war in April 1918. I was fascinated with stories about flying "aces" who engaged in dogfights and thought they were heroes. Germany's "Red Baron" Manfred von Richthofen was probably the best known. Britain's Albert Ball,

James McCudden, and Edward 'Mick' Mannock; South Africa's Andrew Beauchamp-Procter; and Canada's Billy Bishop were all awarded the Victoria Cross for their conspicuous bravery, the highest military award of the British Empire. I had no idea how the Air Force would evolve or the role it would have in twenty years. I had no dreams then of a future in the Air Force or any idea of the part I would play in it.

By the end of the war, Canada had proved its maturity as a nation. Though it was firmly part of the British Empire and Canadians were British subjects, it emerged as a more independent nation. A growing self-confidence was evident in how it dealt with the world.

After the war, my parents felt the loss of friends and family. Those who returned from the war seldom talked about it and many suffered from what was called "shell shock." My father and Uncle Jack Wallace had lost their good friend and brother-in-law, Jimmy Williams. They talked about him but not about the war. I wanted to know more about my father's experience. Once, when I was still quite young, I asked him how he had survived. He paused, thought for a while, and then said, "I don't know how or why I survived through it all. Almost everyone else with me did not."

When we sailed to Canada, my mother was twenty-four, and I was six months old. The plan was that my father would follow soon after. She was returning home, and I was going for the first time. Finding a passage was difficult. However, one was found on a ship that would sail from Liverpool in December. My mother and I took the train there with my nanny, who was to come to Canada with us. At the last minute, the nanny refused to board the ship, fearing the passage across the ocean.

Just as we were about to sail, however, my father was told that he had to remain in England for two more years to attend the Staff College at Sandhurst in Camberley. He sent a wire telling my mother not to sail, but it did not reach us in time. We were already aboard the S.S. *Grampian* and on our way to the Atlantic Ocean.

Our crossing was very rough, but I was unaware of this. Our cabin was in the bowels of the crowded ship. My mother was pregnant and expecting my sister, Jean, and she sometimes suffered from migraine headaches that might knock her out for a few days. As I would learn later, my mother is somewhat fearless, very capable and exceptional at dealing with others. Our ship was a rather small passenger liner of ten thousand tons. Before the war, she had been used on the Montreal to Liverpool route. The following year, 1919, she struck an iceberg off Newfoundland but avoided the *Titanic's* fate, reaching port with no loss of life.

We were part of the enormous demobilization and relocation of people at the end of the War, including 270,000 Canadian soldiers and 54,000 dependents. The logistics were daunting and included almost two million Americans who also had to be brought home across the Atlantic. There were not enough ships for everyone, and many were inadequate.

In Canada, the cost of living rose by 50% from 1916 to 1918 and a general strike that had started in Vancouver continued across the country. It affected dock and railway workers, and winter weather added to the difficulties. Saint John, New Brunswick, and Halifax, Nova Scotia, were the only ice-free Canadian ports available; and Halifax was rebuilding after the massive explosion of 1917 when two ships collided in its harbor, one carrying munitions.

Despite the obstacles, we arrived in Saint John on December 24 and were met by my Canadian grandparents. We all boarded the overnight train and spent Christmas Day traveling to my mother's home, Quebec City. She must have been happy to be there again, but sad to be leaving my father behind in England.

Once the war was over, many officers were discharged because they were no longer needed. The 24th Battalion, Victoria Rifles, was still in England, and my father with them. That Christmas 1918, the Prince of Wales, who would become King Edward VIII, came to visit with my father's regiment, and a few days after Christmas, his brother, Prince Albert, also visited the regiment. My father was assigned to show him around. The prince was only twenty-three and my father described him as "very good-looking, nice, and natural. He looks like the Queen but stands and talks like his father, King George V." Of course, no one at that time expected Prince Albert to become King George VI.

By being selected for the Staff College in Camberley it was more likely that my father would be retained in the peacetime army. He was introduced to a very influential network of military leaders from Britain, Canada, and the rest of the Empire, and he got to know many of them well, which undoubtedly helped him in his military career. Years later, it helped me when I launched my career in the Royal Air Force.

He described his Staff College experience in his journal:

> *A most remarkable gathering. The majority of the 117 students had held commands of battalions. They came from every front. The Royal Navy, Marines, the Army, Royal Flying Corps, Canadians, Australians, New Zealanders, and one South African. Among them were six who had the Victoria Cross (VC), Britain's highest decoration for valor in the presence of the enemy. All had extensive experience, and the majority became generals in their careers.*

The following year, after the course concluded and before returning to Canada, my father spent Christmas with his Aunt Isabel and favorite cousin, Gwen, at Stutton House, the family home in Suffolk. He was very fond of his English family and must have felt sad to be leaving them, wondering when or if he would see them again.

It was his good fortune that he remained in England rather than returning with most of the troops. He had avoided the great influenza that devastated those traveling on ships and trains. The previously unknown virus struck Canada and the United States in waves, and by 1920 it had afflicted 500 million people worldwide and claimed 50 million lives, arriving at ports like Quebec, Montreal, and Halifax. There were no vaccines for protection or antibiotics for treating secondary bacterial infections.

In the United States, there were 670,500 deaths, and in Canada, some 55,000 died, most between the ages of twenty and forty. The death toll added to the 60,000 Canadians who were lost during the war.

On a January morning in 1920, my father's ship sailed up the St. Lawrence River and docked at the port of Quebec. We were living with my grandparents and now were united again. It was then that he saw his baby daughter, Jean, for the first time. She was six months old.

I was two, and my sister was a baby when we moved to Montreal. We lived on Dorchester Street West with our first dog and a nanny who looked after us.

Gertrude with Jimmy and Jean, 1922.

TWO

FIRST LANDING

Being a child with a father in the military, I quickly learned that my parents would never live anywhere for long. When my father arrived, he was assigned immediately as General Staff Officer in Montreal. After a few years in Montreal, we moved to Kingston, Ontario, where he served on the staff of Royal Military College as a professor of military history, organization, strategy, and tactics. After just long enough to become comfortable in the life of the College, we again moved to a new home in Winnipeg, Manitoba, in 1928.

My father spent his youth in England, so he spoke with an English accent. When he took on his assignment in Montreal, he was considered a newcomer to Canada. However, because of his military record and career, he was well respected and had many friends there from before the war.

My mother made friends easily in Montreal, fitting well into the social life my father had to follow with his work. She and my father played badminton often at the Black Watch Armory and she played bridge with her friends. She has always preferred outdoor sports, however, like tennis and horseback riding, and a good game of golf. The garden is still her passion; she treats her flowers like close friends and knows the names of each. She will scold you if you incorrectly pronounce the name of one. On her brisk walks, it can be challenging to keep up with her. My mother can also be quite direct about things and can certainly put her message across. But she does it with humor, and without leaving you uncomfortable. If she notices something, you usually hear about it. When I wore unusual clothing or did something she didn't like, she told me. Her Christian faith has always been important to her; she goes to church on Sundays and says her prayers kneeling beside her bed every night. She loves music and opera and studied it at school in Brussels, Belgium. Like many others, she smokes cigarettes and rolls her own because it is economical. I was often embarrassed at the strings of tobacco hanging from the paper as she lit up and puffed out a great cloud of smoke. She never inhales. Her given name is Gertrude, but my father seldom calls her that because he doesn't like the name. So, he calls her "Peter" instead. I am unsure why; perhaps it is a secret term of endearment.

My father worked long hours and traveled throughout the province of Quebec. He loves the outdoors, and so he rarely turned down an invitation to go hunting in the northern woods. He once told me about going hunting for caribou and moose with a friend from the army named Marcotte. While in his canoe, a beaver swam beside him, and he watched a mother otter teach her young to dive. Walking alone one evening, he encountered a bear and her two cubs. His voice rose about an octave while he talked, and I could tell he'd been frightened.

While his army career is essential to him, he values his outdoor adventures. He loves everything related to nature and is comfortable in it. Fortunately, his military training involves camping and coping with the elements; he seems to thrive on it all. I often wonder if this is what kept him in the military instead of another peacetime occupation.

Although he had worked for a few years at the Bank of Montreal before the war, he had no background in business. He respects the role of government and believes strongly in serving his country, but he has little patience for bureaucracy and paperwork. He likes to get things done.

While living in Montreal, he was never part of the establishment, but he understood it well and felt comfortable among its people. Like him, most families came from Scotland or England and had strong connections to their overseas relatives and friends in Britain.

Montreal at the time was home to Scottish entrepreneurs who had financed and built the railways, resource industries, and banks. He knew many of the leaders of these companies, but he would not have been comfortable in their jobs, and he would never have been an entrepreneur.

Montreal's establishment was English-speaking, yet the city and the province had a majority French-speaking population. In his job, my father was responsible for and worked with the French-speaking regiments and their men. When I was older, I discovered how much they liked and respected him.

Montreal is an island on the St. Lawrence River, distinguished by a large hill called Mount Royal. It was once a volcano. I remember going to Beaver Lake, where we fed the ducks and, in winter, went tobogganing in the snow.

We took the train to Quebec City at Christmas to stay with my grandparents and my mother's family. My Aunt Mary and Uncle Jack Wallace were also there, along with my cousins, Nan and Jackie, who were close to us in age. They lived in Grand-Mère, about eighty miles west of Quebec City. My mother's younger brother, Uncle Sydney, often stayed with us in Montreal. He had graduated from Royal Military College and was completing his chemical engineering degree at McGill University.

When we moved from Montreal to the Royal Military College (RMC), Kingston, Ontario, I was six and Jean was four. I never dreamed that someday I would return there as a cadet.

RMC was established in 1874 by the Canadian parliament to provide a complete education in all branches of military tactics: fortification, engineering, and general scientific knowledge in subjects connected to the military profession. Its graduates served in many conflicts, including the Northwest Rebellion of 1885, the Boer War of 1899-1902, and the Great War of 1914-1918.

Kingston is almost two hundred miles west of Montreal, up the St. Lawrence River on the shore of Lake Ontario. Our home on the RMC campus was frequently filled with cadets because on Sundays, my mother kept an open house and welcomed them for tea or supper. Jean and I thought this was pretty good because the cadets often played fun games with us. Some were from families that my parents knew and three I remember were Kenny Tremain, Tommy MacDougall, and Noel Carrington Smith.

Kingston had plenty of outdoor activities. Jean and I learned to swim there, a skill that would save my life years later. In winter, there was snow, and we often went ice skating on Lake Ontario. Once, I had a bad fall and got a concussion, and one winter, both Jean and I had whooping cough and tonsillitis.

Our parents were both involved in the College, and Jean and I had many friends our age who lived on the campus and whose fathers were on the staff. These were very happy years.

Only later did I appreciate Kingston's history. In 1787 it was called "King's Town" after King George III. Its story is a lesson on military strategy and defense against the threat of invasion. During the War of 1812 between Britain and the United States, an attack across the border would have cut off Upper Canada from Lower Canada and Ontario from Quebec. Thus, an alternate route connecting the two parts of Canada was needed. North of Kingston is a series of lakes. In 1832 they were linked together to become the Rideau Canal. This new waterway linked Kingston to Ottawa and then to Montreal by the Ottawa River. It wasn't until 1867 that the confederation of Canadian provinces joined to become the Dominion of Canada.

My family acquired their first car in 1926, while we were living in Kingston. Driving was a big change for all of us, especially for my parents, who had always depended on horses to get around. It was a Pontiac, and we called it "Sarah." Jean and I loved the "aoogha" sound of its horn or klaxon. Automobiles were appearing on the roads more frequently. Ford made the model "T" and General Motors the Pontiac. According to our parents, the world was changing, but as far as we could tell, our family continued to do things the way they always had. Our parents focused on what they thought needed to be done and were guided by their values. Jean and I played games and sports, and when they had time, our parents played with us. My father was committed to his work at the college and my mother supported him, working on various campus events. They encouraged us in our studies, insisted that we learn how to behave at meals and when meeting others, especially adults. Our possessions were limited to what was considered essential for school and sports. We had books and a few mementos for something we might have achieved. Our clothing was limited to meeting what was considered proper dress. For church on Sundays, I wore a navy-blue blazer, white shirt and tie, grey flannel trousers and black shoes. Of course, my father wore his uniform for different activities and events in which he took part.

I had just turned ten when, in June 1928, he was appointed General Staff Officer in Winnipeg, Manitoba. There, I was sent to Fort Rouge Preparatory School, and Jean attended Rupert's Land College. Our home was on the corner of Wellington Crescent and Academy Road, beside the Assiniboine River.

Very soon, we discovered how different the climate was in Winnipeg. Winters could be very cold, and the northwest winds made it feel even colder. When the snow came, it stayed, and there were seldom thaws. It was an excellent climate for winter sports, and hockey had always been a popular game for people in Winnipeg. Jean and I were often bundled up and sent out to play in the snow, even on very cold days.

My first year at school was hardly an impressive performance. At the end of the first term, I came first in my class, but my report said I was "much too talkative." My report said the same in the spring term, and I came third. In my final term, I came seventh.

My sister Jean was a great success. Not only did she excel in her studies, but like my mother, she loved music and had a very good singing voice that stood her well in her Winnipeg school's singing festival and dramatic productions. In our second year in Winnipeg, I attended St John's School and became a weekly boarder, coming home on weekends. I remember the food most because there was never enough of it. I would ask my parents if they could bring me some of my favorites, and my father would sometimes meet me behind the skating rink and hand me a "grub box." I attended St. John's School for one year and did well. Perhaps it was too easy because I came first in every subject and was described by the headmaster as "a very promising boy."

I was very happy in Winnipeg. Jean and I learned to ride, and we were able to use the horses of the Lord Strathcona Horse Regiment. My father and a few of his friends kept foxhounds and enjoyed the fast and exciting sport of fox hunting. They also hunted large jackrabbits, riding at full gallop on western horses, trying to avoid gopher holes. My father encouraged me to take part in this and he taught me to ride both Western and English saddles and introduced me to jumping. He was very good with horses as was my mother, but he had years of experience with the Army. My mother rode in the Ladies Musical Ride on a Strathcona's horse and she and Jean often rode together. We had our falls and one day when I was riding near a railway an oncoming train whistled; my horse bolted and threw me. I felt a moment of the unknown as I flew through the air, but on landing I wasn't hurt.

I knew little about Winnipeg's past but learned about it later. One of Canada's oldest cities, it had been a busy trading post among the indigenous tribes. It became a trading fort of the French fur traders in 1738 when they connected their trading to the Mississippi River and southward. Living in Winnipeg you knew the importance of the railway. I heard trains whistling night and day. It was at the center of the east-west route of the Transcontinental Railways that carried products across the country and grain from the Prairies to Eastern Canada and to ships sailing abroad. Located 700 miles northwest of Minneapolis, Winnipeg was also known as the "Chicago of the North." Its economic importance began to decline in 1914 when the Panama Canal opened, and shipping took away much of the railways' and Winnipeg's business.

Ronald with his children, Jimmy and Jean, 1924.

Bishop Lennox Waldron Williams and Kara in Tadoussac, Quebec, 1933.

THREE

FAMILY

During the summer of 1930, when I was twelve, my father was required to be at Army Camp. Since he could only join us for a week or two of leave, my mother took us to Quebec for the summer to be with our grandparents.

Her family had been there for almost two centuries since the British had captured Quebec from the French in 1759. My mother's ancestor, Thomas Dunn, arrived in 1760 from Durham, England, immediately following the battle where General James Wolfe had led his troops to victory on the Plains of Abraham. Both Wolfe and the French General, Louis-Joseph de Montcalm were killed, but the battle changed Canada's history. Britain took control of what had been New France.

Like most young boys, I was intrigued by battles, and there are two things I remember about this one: The "Plains" where the battle took place were named after a local farmer called Abraham; and the Fraser Highlanders, who fought for the British, wore their kilts. In the winter months following the battle, they remained in Quebec and had nothing else to wear but those kilts. How did they survive the severe cold? Well, they must have, because that June in 1930 I watched their descendants in their kilts marching on parade along Grande Allée in Quebec.

The story of Quebec embraces you when you are there. It was founded in 1608 by Samuel de Champlain, who dreamed of it being the capital of France's North American Empire. My grandfather told me Quebec is the Algonquin name for "where the river narrows." Here in the St. Lawrence River, where it narrows, the fresh water from the Great Lakes meets the salt and tidal waters from the Atlantic Ocean. When Thomas Dunn (my three-times great-grandfather) arrived there, it was a British fortress inhabited by several British regiments and a growing number of merchants and entrepreneurs who were seeking to make their fortunes from the lumber and agriculture resources, shipping their products overseas from Quebec's year-round seaport.

Thomas Dunn was involved in the St. Maurice Ironworks and other commercial ventures, and he owned lands of the old French seignories along the north shore of the St. Lawrence, where I would spend my summer vacations. He became Civil Administrator of Lower Canada and a Legislative and Executive Councilor. In 1842 his granddaughter, Anne Catherine Dunn (my great-grandmother), met William Rhodes, a young British officer who had been posted to Quebec with his regiment. They fell in love, and what happened next always struck me as a fairy tale. William's family, in Yorkshire, England, soon heard of his relationship with a "colonial" girl. They were horrified and arranged for his regiment to reassign him to Holland. He returned to England but soon resigned from his commission and returned to Quebec to marry his love. This must have taken considerable courage because he was the second son in his family, and under English common law and custom, he would not inherit any of his family's estate. It would go to his older brother. His career as an officer in the army would be his primary livelihood and would provide the social status he needed in England. Instead, he chose to seek a new life in the colonies, where he knew almost no one. He and Anne Catherine Dunn were married and, in time, became prominent members of the Quebec and Lower Canada community. They had five sons and four daughters, one of whom, Caroline Anne, was my grandmother. William Rhodes died long before I was born, but my first memory of him was my grandmother telling me he had introduced strawberries to Quebec and grew seven acres of them on his farm. I love strawberries and when I was ten, I was convinced that my great-grandfather had done something very important. The strawberries from Quebec are the best I have ever tasted.

William Rhodes, frequently called "the Colonel," loved the wild country. He spent so much time in it that he was described by Fennings Taylor, the historical biographer, as "the great northern hunter." On his trips to hunt caribou or moose he was often accompanied by Cornelius Krieghoff, the Dutch painter, famous for his many winter scenes of early Canada. My great grandfather appears in some of them. He was a member of the Assembly of Lower Canada, and in 1854, Minister of Agriculture and Colonel of the Militia. He founded a bank, a warehousing company and was president of several railways and the Quebec Bridge Company. He actively promoted the first bridge across the St. Lawrence River in 1867 while John A. MacDonald (the Prime Minister) was pulling Canada together into a Confederation. His outdoor interests led him northeast by boat from Quebec City, 150 miles along the St. Lawrence River to an old settlement at the mouth of the Saguenay River called Tadoussac. At 48.14 degrees latitude and 9.7128 longitude, it is almost 700 miles north of New York City. This little settlement was where the French explorer, Jacques Cartier, landed in 1535 on his first voyage to the New World. In 1603, Samuel de Champlain arrived in Tadoussac on the first of his 23 voyages from France. He established what today is one of the oldest European settlements in North America. By the time I came there, more than three hundred years later, there was still lots of fishing, and logging operations by the Price family, however, the Hudson's Bay Company's trading post was gone.

In 1858, Col. Rhodes was looking for a place where he and his family could enjoy the sea air during the summers and where they could fish, camp, boat, and explore the rugged country and seaside. He decided to build a house looking over the beautiful bay in Tadoussac. His good friend, Willis Russell, also from Quebec, built a home beside him. They helped establish a community of families that have been spending their summers in Tadoussac ever since.

At the end of June, after seeing my grandparents in Quebec, my mother took Jean and me to the Rhodes family house in Tadoussac. My grandparents left for a visit to England, but our cousins, Nan and Jackie Wallace, were there with us, and my father was able to get leave to join us in August. He arrived just in time because, a few days later, my mother went to Quebec City and my brother Ronnie was born on August 27. We were twelve years apart in age, and while I felt very close to my sister, I was now excited to have a brother.

That Autumn my father went to England to see his family and he returned with two Samoyed dogs. They were beautiful, furry, and pure white and they added so much to our family. Each had long pedigrees. One came from Shackleton's dogs in the Antarctic, and the other was descended from dogs on Scott's Antarctic expedition. My Aunt Isabel at Stutton in Suffolk, England had bred Samoyeds. My father may have planned it, but our two dogs, Nick and Galka, would soon begin their own dynasty of Samoyeds. My parents bred them for years and Galka had thirty pups. She came second in the Open at Madison Square Garden. Some of the pups remained in the family. My mother's father, "the Bishop," had Kara, and my parents kept a pup for themselves. They called him Peter, which must have been confusing when my father also called my mother Peter.

Notwithstanding his time in Canada, England was always in my father's thoughts, and he often talked about his childhood and the times he spent there with his many aunts, uncles, and cousins. My father felt strongly that Britain had done such good for the world. His views influenced me, and I wondered whether I should consider myself British or Canadian. Was it a choice I would make? My father became a Canadian, and despite his English accent, he was very comfortable among his many Canadian friends and acquaintances. He had a keen interest in the affairs of Canada and a passion for its beauty and wildlife. However, his visits to England were very important to him. He grew up away from his parents, who lived in Ceylon while he was in England.

My grandfather, John Abercromby Alexander, was Scottish and the eldest of four boys and three girls, but he was never close to any of his siblings. As a young man, he had left his family in Peebles, Scotland, to work in Ceylon. The blight of the 1870s, which destroyed coffee plantations across Ceylon, presented an opportunity for English plantation owners to replace coffee by planting tea. This required extensive cutting of the forests, a perfect job for a young man.

My grandfather learned about biology, and as they developed the new tea plantations, he studied the variety of plant life in the subtropical climate of Ceylon. He became the Chief Forester and a well-known botanist, and his photograph collection of different plants and their cultivation is at Cambridge University. My father described him as "a fine-looking man, over six feet tall, very erect, and looking, like a Scottish chieftain." At age ten, my father and his younger brother, Tim, were taken by their mother to school in England. During their holidays and summers, they went to Turnworth, her family home in Dorset.

My grandmother, Mary Parry Okeden, came from an English family. Her father had served as a magistrate with the British Civil Service in India, and she was one of thirteen children. In 1885, young, unmarried and in her early thirties, she set out alone on a voyage from England across the world that included a visit to a friend living in Ceylon. She sailed to Gibraltar, made stops at Malta and Alexandria, going ashore for a game of tennis or a garden party at the Governor's mansion. Her ship passed through the Suez Canal and the Red Sea into the Gulf of Aden and across the Indian Ocean, arriving in Colombo. She remained in Ceylon for almost a year, most of the time in the hills around the tea plantations. While there, she made many friends and met a Mr. Alexander. Her travels continued to India and on her return to England, again passing through the Suez Canal, she spent several months in Florence, Italy. Shortly after arriving back in England, she received a letter from Mr. Alexander requesting her hand in marriage. She returned to Ceylon, was married there in 1886 and lived in Kandy, where my father was born. According to him, she was a devout Christian, loved to act, sing and to play tennis. He described her as "short, plump, even-tempered and very sympathetic." She spent most of her married life in Ceylon, but she maintained close ties with her brothers and sisters in England. Uncle Uvedale, the eldest, had inherited the family home at Turnworth in Dorset. Uncle Billy served as a judge in Rangoon and Uncle Herbert owned the estate in Suffolk called Stutton House. His wife, Aunt Isabel, was very good to my father and he often stayed with them. Their daughter, Gwen St. John, was his first cousin, and they were like brother and sister. Gwen's only son, Julian, was tragically killed in an automobile accident in 1936. Had he lived, he would have inherited the beautiful Stutton House and estate. This meant that at some time in the future it was likely to be left to me.

My grandmother Alexander spent much of her childhood with her large family. Her parents had a home in London at 61 Cornwall Gardens, South Kensington, but it was at Turnworth, the stately manor in Dorset, where the family gathered. Thomas Hardy had featured Turnworth in his novel, *The Woodlanders*.

My father, who spent his summer holidays there in the beautiful English countryside, once described it to me:

> *It was a life that no longer exists. The house had about twenty bedrooms, with night and day nurseries. The finest rooms were downstairs; the library had a lovely old, vaulted ceiling. In the large kitchen, copper pans and utensils were hanging from the walls. There were no bathrooms; only one W.C. (water closet) downstairs for the men and one upstairs for the women which was called the 'lending library' because it had a bookcase. The house was heated by open fireplaces, although there were tin baths in the bedrooms. At night, light was provided by oil lamps downstairs and candles in the bedrooms. Family prayers were held every evening. Everyone including the servants were required to attend.*

His memories of his cousins, aunts and uncles were the happiest gifts of his childhood, and he often shared them with me. I felt sure that someday, although I lived in Canada, I would get to know them. He was teaching me the meaning of family and friends and, during times of stress and uncertainty in the future, I would find strength in this. My entire upbringing was in Canada, surrounded by my Canadian family and I did not meet and know my father's family until I returned to England at age twenty-one to join the RAF. When my grandparents retired, they left Ceylon and returned to live in Parkstone, England. My grandmother Alexander died in 1925, at age seventy-five and my parents sailed to England. My grandfather Alexander met them at the railway station. He had a cold, which got worse, and he died a few days later at age seventy-seven. He was buried beside my grandmother in Poole, Dorset.

Jimmy, 1930.

Jimmy, Jean and Ronnie, 1934.

FOUR

SCHOOL YEARS

At the end of that summer in 1930, I did not return to Winnipeg. My parents had other plans for me. When I was born, my father had decided to secure a place for me at Wellington College, a boarding school in Berkshire, England. As the years passed, his postwar experience in Canada must have changed his mind, and he and my mother decided instead that I should attend a Canadian boarding school.

In early September my father delivered me to Bishop's College School in Lennoxville, Quebec. I was twelve years old. All the students were boarders and during the school year we lived at the school, except for Christmas and Easter holidays, when I could return home to Winnipeg.

Lennoxville is a small town located about 100 miles south of Montreal in an area known as the Eastern Townships. The school, known as BCS, was founded in 1836 and sits on a hill beside the beautiful St. Francis River. Every morning, on that hill behind the school, a steam engine from the old Grand Trunk Railway would wake us with its "good morning" whistle as it hauled its load up the steep grade. We wondered if it would make it. The railway was built in 1853 and ran between Montreal and Portland, Maine.

On opening day, my father dropped me off at school and wished me well. I felt badly for him, remembering that his mother had taken him and his brother from Ceylon and left them at school in

England when he was only ten. He needn't have worried about me. I was excited about coming to BCS and I had been well prepared by members of my family who had been there before me.

My great-grandfather on my mother's side, James W. Williams, had come from Wales to be the third headmaster of BCS from 1857 to 1863. He was an ordained minister, with an MA from Pembrooke College, Oxford, and he later became Bishop of Quebec. His son, my grandfather, Lennox Williams, was born in Chapman House, once the headmaster's residence. He later attended the school and was Head Prefect. I knew that he and my grandmother were pleased that I was going to BCS. Her five brothers, Armitage, Godfrey, William, Francis, and Robert Rhodes were at BCS during the 1860s and 70s. One or two of them would have been classmates of the sons of Jefferson Davis, the President of the Confederacy during the American Civil War. When the Davis family moved to Montreal after the war, Jeff Davis Jr. and William Davis went to BCS.

I found my first few days at the school bewildering, but not for long. I learned there was a schedule for everything and a routine for getting things done. Bells would ring and punctuality was enforced. I soon got to know my classmates and we realized we were all in this together. We slept in large dorms on small iron-post beds; there were thirteen boys in my dorm. For my first year, we were in the Preparatory School where the youngest classes occupied a separate section of the main buildings, which was referred to as the "Upper School." It wasn't clear what we were being prepared for, but we felt that the Upper School was the real one because it was bigger. The school buildings were formidable, made of red brick covered with ivy, and green playing fields sloped away in front of them.

We ate our meals with the boys from the Upper School in the grand dining hall that was connected by a cloister to the main building. The gymnasium was also located there. The Upper School boys wore jackets and ties. We in the Prep wore our purple sweaters, the school color. On Sundays we wore purple blazers, grey flannel trousers, and a purple and white striped Prep School tie. Each morning a wake-up bell rang at 7:15. Morning prayers followed breakfast before classes began. Sports began at 3P.M.: soccer in autumn, hockey and skiing in winter, and cricket in spring. After dinner, it was back to the classroom for homework, called prep, followed by milk and soda biscuits before bed and lights out.

A prayer light in our dorm stayed on while we knelt beside our beds to say our prayers. On Saturdays, we had morning classes followed by afternoon sports and sometimes a reading or film in the evening.

Sunday morning was church, but the rest of the day we could ride bikes or play in the woods surrounding the school. I soon discovered that the hill was suitable for skiing in winter and hiking in spring and fall. The deep woods around the school were ideal for unofficial war games and picnics on Sunday evenings in log cabins which some of the boys had built.

The Prep school had a matron to look after us. Miss Reyner was nurturing but firm; we all liked her very much. She considered it her job to prepare us for our move to the Upper School. She helped us to pack and unpack our trunks, inspecting the clothing lists to ensure we had the right clothes to take home for the holidays. It was a long way home to Winnipeg, but I was very excited to leave for the holidays and when the morning came for me to take the train to Montreal, I would stand waiting on the station platform anxiously looking for the large steam engine that would pull the train into Lennoxville for us to board. When we arrived in Montreal I had to change to another train for a full day and night journey to Winnipeg.

During that first year, I learned the real meaning of discipline. I associated it with the Army because of my father, but at school there was a schedule for almost every hour. This was new to me, as was the discipline of following it. I soon found it easy to work with because I learned to be prepared for the demands made on us and how to meet them. If you think ahead, get done what needs doing, especially doing first what you don't like, then the time left is free and seems to be worth more. I was enjoying the school and did well in my studies, except for history. I played sports and made new friends, mostly from Montreal and a few from Quebec City.

At school we were totally focused on our daily life and by school closing in June, we were ready to enjoy our summer holidays. We were unaware of the events happening in the financial world and how they would change lives, including my own.

When I returned to BCS for the 1931-32 school year, there were only 72 boys, the smallest number in years. Some of my classmates were missing because their parents had lost their savings and could not afford to pay the school's tuition fees. My parents explained the general situation, but I did not understand how it might affect us.

At school, our first concern was the loss of classmates. Some had become good friends. I continued to worry who else among us would have to leave because of circumstances their parents were facing. Our teachers did not discuss it; we guessed they were also worried. At morning assembly, prayers were said for the unemployed and the poor. In time, we learned that on "Black Monday," October 1929, the New York Stock Exchange had dropped 13%. It was to lose 89% of its value over the next three years.

In our history class, our teacher sometimes would tell us what he had read in the *Montreal Gazette*. Canada was being hit hard because products from our mining, lumber, fishing, and agricultural industries weren't being exported to the United States and Britain. My father was one of the fortunate ones: as an officer in the Army, he was able to keep his job.

At school, we seldom talked about what our fathers did for work. One of my classmates who had to leave school told me that his family's business was "having difficulty." Another said his father worked for the Bell Telephone Company who would "look after him."

I felt depressed at times, like everyone else, but the full plate of school activities that demanded my attention usually lifted my spirits. And then my father told me the bad news: he had kept his job in the Army, but his salary had never been enough to pay my tuition at BCS. He explained that he and my mother had counted on their savings to send me to school:

> *The stock market was booming, and we were doing very well. To build up our capital to pay for your education I did what thousands of others were doing. I bought stocks on margin in a booming market. When I look back on my life and consider that I had always been careful and conservative, I can't imagine why I ever did anything so rash and stupid. When the crash came thousands were ruined. Not only did I lose practically all the capital which I had inherited from my mother, but also your mother's money.*

He told me how strong my mother was about it all, which of course she would be. He said, *"as always, she took it on the chin."*

Telling me what happened could not have been easy for him. Fortunately, I was able to remain at the school because my grandparents were willing and able to pay for my tuition. However, I would not be able to return home for my holidays, because it would be too expensive for my father and my mother to pay for my travel to Winnipeg.

I was not sure what to think. Holidays at home were what made boarding school tolerable. My sister, Jean, was at school in Winnipeg. She and my little brother, Ronnie, would be with my mother and father. I could not imagine how I would get on without them. I felt much better when I realized that I could spend my

Christmas and Easter holidays with my grandparents in Quebec City, an easy train ride from the school.

This was a turning point in my teenage years. I loved my parents, sister, and brother deeply, and the feeling of separation left a deep pit in my stomach. However, I was soon to discover the good fortune awaiting me.

My school had rather curious ways based on British traditions. When we moved up from the Prep to the Upper school, we became "new boys," which seemed a bit odd, but the "new boy" system had been embedded in British schools for half a century. Although fagging, which involved running errands for seniors, had been discontinued some years before, the prefects still enforced discipline and punishment. They were permitted to use caning when students broke the rules. There were special rules for new boys: no hands in pockets, no use of center stairs, address older boys by their surnames, and no running in the corridors. Before all meals, new boys had to stand in a long line, tallest on the right, shortest on the left, for inspection. Punishment was given if we were not properly dressed in tie and jacket with well-polished shoes and clean fingernails. No elbows could be on the table at meals, and butter could not be wasted or left on our plates. At all school games, we had to cheer together loudly.

Outside of our studies, there was a wide selection of activities. I joined the Photography Club, learned to develop and print film, and carried a camera whenever allowed. Writing was also considered an essential activity, and I was fortunate to have Lewis Evans, a young English composition teacher, who had recently come to the school. I met him in Tadoussac during the summer where his family had a cottage. He encouraged me to write, and I soon wrote weekly reports on the football and hockey games we played against other schools. It was my first and only experience as a sports reporter, but I learned to love poetry, and he encouraged me to put into verse what I saw and felt about life, including life at school.

Sports were strongly encouraged, and it was compulsory to play at least one sport every term. I loved hockey and football and enjoyed tennis, but I was especially keen on team sports. We had good instruction on how to play and had frequent practices on weekdays and Saturdays. We competed seriously with other schools. Sometimes we won and sometimes we lost. Good sportsmanship was stressed above all else. In winning, modesty and humility should guide how we conducted ourselves. If we personally scored or were cheered for something we had done, we should not celebrate but quietly acknowledge the support of our teammates and the school. When we lost, we were to cheer and congratulate our opponents for their good play or good luck. In team games we were taught that it was the team that was most important, that we were playing for our team and our teammates, not for ourselves as individuals. I discovered that when my teammates gave their best, I wanted to do the same and if one scored or made an exceptional play I felt very good for him.

I played hockey almost every day. Our team often played against St. Pat's, the Catholic school in the nearby city of Sherbrooke. We played on outside ice and in January, it could be fiercely cold, and often we froze our ears. There might also be a warming thaw which could turn the ice into a pond. At the St. Pat's rink, the loudspeakers would blare out a Viennese waltz, as if we were about to perform a ballet. The referees were priests who taught at St. Pat's and wore their black cassocks on the ice. On the days that we weren't playing hockey I went skiing and found some good runs on the hills behind the school.

BCS was a Christian school. Most of the boys were from Protestant families, some were Roman Catholic, and a few were

Jewish, and all but a few spoke English as their mother tongue. Every morning before classes began, we would gather in the assembly hall for prayers and to sing a hymn. On Sundays, chapel was held at St. Mark's on the campus of Bishop's University, an easy walk from the school. I sang in the choir, first as a treble and when my voice broke, as a bass. The choir wore red cassocks with white surplices over them at both Mattins and Evensong. It was a very good choir, with excellent instruction in four-part harmony and capable of singing some of the best of English choral music. We were taught like an English choir to pronounce the hard 'a' as an 'o' when we sang the hymns, canticles and anthems. The choir practiced twice every week.

The school placed a high value on its traditions and its history. The old boys who had served during the Great War were examples, and many were fresh in the memories of those who now taught us. We were inspired and awed by the stories we heard about them and their photographs hung on the hallway walls. Some had been awarded the Victoria Cross for their bravery and courage in saving their comrades. The BCS magazine celebrated them one year with the heading, *"Dulce et decorum est, pro patria mori."* Translated from Latin, it means, "It is sweet and glorious to die for one's Country." On November 11, we observed Remembrance Day, and a special guard from our cadet corps led all boys from the school to the cenotaph in Lennoxville for a brief service to remember those killed during the war. Their names were read aloud, including my Uncle James Williams. I thought of him and my father's experience in the Great War. I was always moved by this ceremony, which was concluded by the bugle playing the Last Post.

BCS has a long tradition in its cadet corps and every boy in the school had to become a cadet. During the Great War, 269 former BCS cadets volunteered for active service; 66 were killed. The old militia uniforms had been retired, and our Headmaster, Crawford Grier, introduced the formal blues with brass buttons and pillbox caps. The cadet corps was the smartest looking in Canada, and when on parade, the BCS No. 2 Cadet Corps marched with its battle colors, which it earned from its service in 1865 during the Fenian Raids on Canada. Our brass buttons shone almost white; our black boots, spats, and leather belts glittered and reflected the light. Preparing for a parade took a serious effort, which might be avoided if "new boys" who had broken school rules were given the punishment of cleaning belts and boots and shining the brass. Not everyone enjoyed our cadet experience, but I learned from it and was able to train and qualify as a marksman. The school had a long tunnel under the main building, and at one end was the rifle range.

My studies went well during my first few years at BCS. I had good marks in English, Mathematics, and Science but received average marks for French and history. We got to know most of our teachers well and often had special names for them. My science teacher was called "Plush" Pattison. I never understood why because he had little appearance of the luxurious. He had a dry sense of humor and would test us with quizzes, such as "Why are there as many odd numbers as there are numbers?"

At the end of each term, we looked forward to the holidays, or as some said, "getting out of jail," but it was never over until we finished writing our exams. Here is a poem I wrote about exams:

Terror fills my heart.
Exams are very near
Have I learned my part?
Is my constant fear.

On my fourth year at the school, I did poorly on my exams, and it was not unusual to be reprimanded. The headmaster wrote "unsatisfactory" on my report and said, "I look for harder work from him next year. I fear he is attempting too much." I didn't agree. I was involved in many activities, but this wasn't the reason.

I had discovered something new. It all began in Quebec City over the Christmas and New Year holidays in 1933-34.

I missed my parents and Jean and Ronnie. I hadn't seen them since the end of the summer and wouldn't be likely to see them until the following summer. However, I was excited to go to Quebec City to be with my grandparents again. The atmosphere in Quebec is magical and very festive at Christmas time. There is always snow, and lots of it after a snowstorm. I loved to walk at night through the streets of this old walled city. The stone houses were decorated with reflecting candlelight that celebrated Christmas and told of the warmth inside each home. The tall spruce trees were laden with snow, and as I walked along the snow-covered streets the jingle of sleigh bells announced another team of horses pulling their sleigh over the snow on the roads around the city center. Riding in a sleigh is the best way to get around, especially after a heavy snowfall. It can also be very cold with a strong wind off the river, so you need to bundle up. When you first step outside, the cold can take your breath away.

My grandparents lived at Bishopthorpe, the residence of the Bishop of the Anglican Diocese of Québec, near St. Louis Gate, which was built originally by the French during the 17th century as an entry to the walled city. It is near the Cathedral of Holy Trinity, where I went with my grandparents on Sundays and Christmas Day. I was inspired by the architecture inside the cathedral, the Ionic columns and its beautiful ceiling, and the Christmas music was wonderful with the large pipe organ and perfect acoustics. The cathedral was completed in 1804 and modeled after St. Martin-in-the-Fields in London. It was in the center of town, close to all the action and to the Chateau Frontenac, where many holiday celebrations were held. One of our favorite places was the amazing toboggan slide constructed beside the hotel, looking over the river.

My friends and I would climb up to the top and race each other down. The hotel was built in 1893 by the Canadian Pacific Railway and named after Frontenac, the Governor of New France. It dominates the high point of the city, looking over the St. Lawrence River. Many of the buildings are in the early French style, made of grey stones, with sloping roofs, small windows, and very thick walls to protect against the cold winter winds. The city is at its best in winter. The light glitters brightly on the snow on sunny days, but it is cold outside. The wood fires burning inside give warmth and remind one of the very hard life the early *habitants* faced from the time Quebec was established by Samuel de Champlain in 1608.

Christmas with my grandparents was a family time. Many of my grandmother's relatives lived in Quebec, and I saw them, but the most fun was being with my first cousins, who also came for Christmas. Aunt Mary and Uncle Jack Wallace were there with my cousins, Nan and Jackie, and their younger brother, Michael, who was close in age to my brother, Ronnie. Uncle Sydney and Aunt Enid Williams were there with my cousins, Joan and Susan. There are things we all share and remember about Christmas, and I will never forget that at eleven o'clock on Christmas morning, everything stopped. We listened in awe to His Majesty King George V's voice on the radio. It was a highlight of the day.

The first time this happened was at Christmas in 1932. For so many in Canada and from all parts of the British Empire it was the first time they had ever heard him speak. It became a tradition that would continue every year. George V served as King of Great Britain, the British Dominions and as Emperor of India from 1910 to 1936. His Majesty was the symbol of the British Empire and a very special person who dedicated his life to the interests and care of his people in all parts of the world. He was a grandson of Queen Victoria. I was always fascinated that his first cousins were Tsar Nicholas II of Russia and Kaiser Wilhelm II of Germany and that all three of them led their countries during the Great War.

During the Christmas and New Years holidays in Quebec I spent most of my time with my family and my cousins, in particular; but the 1933/34 holidays were different. Being a teenager and almost sixteen, I was invited to many parties over the holidays, often with dinner and dancing well into the night. I had made good friends in Quebec, among them, Ted Price, who I knew from our summers together in Tadoussac. He went to Trinity College School (TCS) in Port Hope, Ontario for a while, but was at home with his large Price family in Quebec at Christmas. Ted always stood out at a party with his red hair.

He loved everyone, had a good laugh and was always fun to be with. Mac Clarke, my classmate at BCS, lived in Quebec as did tennis friends Helen Neilson and Ann Fisher. I knew Helen from our summers. Ann lived in Sackville, New Brunswick, but came to Quebec frequently to see her grandparents. She spent summers at St. Patrick on the south shore of the St. Lawrence River. The big difference that year was the girls, the parties and the dancing.

Girls have always been a mystery to me. I loved my sister and cousins but went to an all-boys school. At the parties and dances in Quebec, I felt quite different about the girls I was meeting. I found them intriguing and attractive. At the Winter Club dance, I met a girl called Janet Gibault. I saw her again at another dance held by the Clarkes. These were the only times I saw her during the Christmas holidays, but when I danced with her, I experienced a spell I had never felt before.

She had dark hair, almost silky black, dark eyes and a smooth complexion. Afterward, I wanted to ring her on the phone, but I thought it would be so hopeless, and I might annoy her and spoil any chance I might have. I liked many of the other girls I met, especially Barbara Billington and Sheila Power. The parties continued after Christmas, and we met for tea at the Chateau Frontenac or lunch at Kent House beside Montmorency Falls. The falls are 100 feet higher than Niagara Falls but much narrower. On New Year's Eve, we were all out at the Citadel together. I was with Sheila Power and got to bed at 4:30 A.M. The next night, we were at Archie Cooke's, and I took Sheila home.

Yet I seemed caught in a cloud thinking about Janet. She lived on Grande Allée at the far end of the Plains of Abraham. I saw Sheila again at parties the next few nights, and four of us went to see a movie. There were parties every day, including lunches and a tea dance. At the end of the week, I took Sheila back to her Convent school. I went skiing at Lake St. Charles, and the next day, I had lunch at Benmore, my Rhodes family home. It was my grandmother's birthday. After two weeks of fun, family, and friends I returned to school on the Quebec Central Railroad.

When I look back and remember this time, I realize I was in a fog; I couldn't understand why. After leaving Quebec, I was spellbound about the girls I had got to know, Janet Gibault, in particular. Soon after I had returned to school, I received a letter from Janet's girlfriend asking me to write to Janet, saying she was apparently "lovesick" over me. Wow! I had been dying to write to her, but I didn't know how to get started. So, I wrote, and she wrote back to me. This continued for a couple of months. I had a letter from Sheila Power, and I wrote to her and to Barbara Billington. Letter writing from school was a frequent activity, but usually it was to parents or family. Writing long letters to girls, especially if you feel madly in love, is very time-consuming. I wrote letters during French classes and evening study sessions. I waited anxiously for Janet's replies, but they were slow to come. I wished I could stop thinking about her because it was a kind of torture. After waiting a long time without receiving a letter from her, I was desperate. Then, a letter from her sister came explaining that Janet had been in the hospital with appendicitis. When her letters arrived, I was ecstatic; when they didn't, I was in pain. My studies were suffering. When I returned to Quebec City for my Easter holidays in April,

I was excited to see Janet again and loved going around with her that week, but I wasn't sure she felt the same about me.

Once I was back at school again for the final term of the year, I played cricket almost every day, and with the Cadet Corps, we prepared for the annual inspection and parade. I was involved in boxing matches, singing in the choir, and writing poetry. When the weather was warmer, we swam in the St. Francis River. Sometimes, dances were organized with King's Hall, Compton, the girls' boarding school nearby, and at one of these dances, I was rather taken with one of the girls, but I was able to resist adding her to my already busy list of girls to write letters to.

I was trying to establish my credentials and confidence with girls. Letters from Janet were less frequent now. I wrote to Teddy Price because I suspected it was his fault that Janet wasn't writing to me. He was going to school in Quebec City this year. Janet's next letter was somewhat cool with lots about Teddy. I wrote to Sheila. A week later, a letter from Janet arrived, and I wrote in my diary, "We are through, and I was right. It is Teddy. I don't care. I'll get her back. You just watch and see."

During those first six months of 1934, I kept a diary with full details of what I was doing at school, including the letters I wrote to everyone, especially the girls. At the end of 1934, I made a note reflecting on the year in my diary. During that winter term, January through March 1934, I came 10th out of 16 in my class, and I got 16 out of 100 in history. The reason was apparent, and my diary explained it:

> *When I wrote to Janet it was on the off chance that she would write to me. Consequently, I was still writing to Sheila and Barbara when I got Janet's nice letter. It took a little while for me to get up the nerve to break it off with Sheila and in the end I did. I did not break it off with Barb, but I did not two-time Janet as the letters which I wrote to Barb where*

brotherly letters and had none of the feelings in them that were in the ones to Janet.

At Easter, someone told me I had better write to Sheila or Sheila would break down. I know how I would feel if I were her so I think I will have to, but it will be difficult without two timing Janet. However, I will do my best. Then on May 2nd, Janet broke it off saying she'd fallen for Ted (Price). Best of luck Ted! I may go back to Sheila, but I don't know. We'll see what happens!

The spring term at school always seemed to generate more energy. We were back outside for sports, and the days were longer. It is a refreshing season as the leaves burst out, giving new life. The weather was usually good, with some rain and more sun, but still quite cool. On May 24, we celebrated Queen Victoria's birthday with fireworks. She died in 1901, and her birthday is a holiday throughout the British Empire. At the annual Sunday Church Parade in Montreal, it was a tradition for the BCS cadet Corps to be represented, and I marched as a member of our color party. I stayed overnight with Aunt Mary and Uncle Jack Wallace, and I was able to see my cousin Jackie. Back at school, tennis became a favorite, and I began to play competitively. I got to the finals, played against my classmate, Mac Clarke, and won the singles tournament. Mac and I had also played on the first Hockey team together.

In September 1934, at sixteen, I began my final year. My school years were good years, but at times, I deeply missed my family. My sister and I were very close, and we had done many things together. Until I went to BCS we were seldom apart. I also missed Ronnie and knew he was growing up fast. I looked forward to when my mother would bring them east for the summers. My father was always away at military camp and joined us only for a short time. I did not see much of him during my teenage years, but he wrote letters to me often, and when we were together, he wanted to hear what I was doing and what I was thinking. During our conversations, I became aware of his belief in discipline and the importance of character. Being "on time" was part of his military life, but he also expected it from his family.

He was clear about what he considered was right or wrong – and he would speak directly about it. Sometimes he sounded severe, but we got used to it. He was really very kind. On alcohol, he said it was all right to drink but not to excess, and certainly not if it was going to affect your behavior or ability to carry out your duties. We talked about my future and what I might do after finishing school at BCS. The dominant choices were to attend McGill University in Montreal or if I were accepted, go to Royal Military College in Kingston, Ontario. The prospect of military college was not new to me. I remembered living there and many of my relatives and family friends had gone to RMC.

I enjoyed my five years at BCS and will be forever grateful for the education it gave me, not just in my studies but also in teamwork, games, sportsmanship, and self-discipline. The school offered a great choice of activities and sports. I made the most of them and made life-long friendships with my classmates. You get to know people very well when you live with them day and night for several years. I managed to finish well.

I overcame my infatuation with girls and studied hard. I came first in my class at Christmas and continued my efforts throughout the year. I played on the first teams in ice hockey, football, and cricket and won the tennis cup and a gold medal in gymnastics and shooting. I was also a sergeant in the Cadet Corps. My interest in photography became a serious hobby, and I was involved in the school press. I also continued to write poetry.

I am very grateful for the opportunity I had. We were brought up to believe that if we gave our best, it would benefit not only us but others as well. We were taught never to promote ourselves. Boasting was considered extremely bad form, and we had to trust that others would discover what we did and were able to do. To talk negatively of someone else was also not done. If they were doing something wrong, in time it would be found out. Telling or "squealing" on them was the worst. Praise for others was encouraged, but it had to be honest. Our values in life were founded on the belief that the common good should come before our own individual actions and achievements.

Entrance to university required us to sit for matriculation exams in each subject administered by McGill University. I wrote them in June and then waited anxiously for the results. My final days at school were filled with happy emotions. I had made such good friends, and now we would go our separate ways, each taking a different path to the future. I expressed my feelings in one of my poems, a sonnet:

> *No power can wipe out, or ever will,*
> *The mem'ry of our school, where tolled the gong*
> *Of loyalty and honor. T'will be strong*
> *Within our hearts, forever there to fill*
> *A place aside. All wishing we were still*
> *Beneath her wing, amidst the youthful throng.*
> *Where side-by-side we fought: we stayed not long;*
> *For soon we left our home upon the hill–*
> *For the great task in life that's for us set*
> *And if despair and failure there are met;*
> *The spirit of our school we'll still retain,*
> *To urge us on, and never to regret,*
> *A power with us ever to remain:*
> *The honor of our school we'll ne'er forget.*

When the exam results were announced: I led my class on the McGill matric exams, scoring 100 in both elementary algebra and geometry, 97 in Intermediate Trigonometry, 76 in Intermediate Algebra, 92 in Chemistry, and 86 in Physics. I won the Governor General's Medal with the Greenshields Memorial Scholarship to McGill University by coming first in my class. However, I had now decided to go to RMC, and if accepted, the scholarship to McGill would go to the student who came second in my class. My other prizes included the Old Boy's Prize, the Geo. R. Hooper Prize for mathematics, and the Edgar Black Prize for science. Curiously, my lowest marks were in English literature, composition, and French. I returned to the school at the annual prize giving the following September.

My parents were there, and my grandfather had been invited to hand out the prizes. It is hard to describe how I felt receiving them from him. I hoped that he and my parents might feel some reward for the encouragement and guidance they had given me. The prizes I received were beautiful leather-bound books: Liddell Hart's *Scipio Africanus*, *T.E Lawrence in Arabia*, and *Foch, The Man of Orleans*. Others were *South with Scott*, *Abraham Lincoln*, *Robert E. Lee*, *Stonewall Jackson* and *The Great Physician* about Sir William Osler, *the History of Agriculture* and *Seven Pillars of Wisdom* by T.E. Lawrence.

I must have finished on good grounds with the Headmaster, Crawford Grier, who wrote this in his report: "A splendid result; we shall watch Jim's career at RMC with great interest. BCS needs good men there." Mr. Grier took a continuing interest in my progress through RMC when I attended flying school after graduation and joined the Royal Air Force in 1940.

My years at BCS were behind me. I was pleased about the good memories and the many friends I had made, and the thought of crossing a bridge into a new and bigger world was uplifting. My application to RMC had been submitted, but I was waiting to receive official notice that I had been accepted. I knew the chances were good, so I wasn't very worried, but there is always that element of doubt in waiting. It was time to enjoy the summer.

During my years at BCS when I spent my summers at Tadoussac with my grandparents, I grew to appreciate how much they had done for me. Of course, I was grateful that they had paid for my schooling, but they gave me so much more. They treated me as an adult and expected me to behave as one, giving me support and confidence along the way. I realized how much I loved them both and will never forget the greeting they gave me any time I arrived at their home.

My grandfather would spread his arms and joyfully reach out for a welcome embrace. He had a melodious laugh and a grand smile. He stood tall and straight and wore his white clerical collar. His voice was strong and clear, commanding only when it needed to be, such as when giving a sermon. His hair was grey, almost white, and he wore a full beard which felt prickly when I kissed him, something I always did when I saw him or when saying good night. He smoked a pipe at times, and when you were close to him you would get that sweet aroma of his very good tobacco. When he walked you could hear him coming, his feet pounding the floor or the stairs. I was told he had flat feet, but this never prevented him from being a very good athlete. He loved sports and took care of himself to be in good physical condition and he was always active.

Grannie had a playful sense of humor. She had lots of energy and was always game for fun. She could be firm, but she had a warm smile and a confident presence with everyone. When I was very young, I remember looking up at her smiling face. She was not tall at just over five feet, and it wasn't long before I grew taller and looked down at the top of her head. When I was in Quebec one Easter, I had taken some photos to be developed but had returned to school without them. I then wanted the negatives so I could create some interesting prints. I wrote a letter to Grannie saying that I had left the films in her name at the Frontenac shop, and I asked her to get them for me, which she did. She was always thinking of me. Often, she would send me money to spend at the Tuck shop for candy bars and other sweets. I would write to thank her for the money and for the cake she had sent, saying it was delicious and then I would hint that she might send me some of Morgan's chocolate eclairs and possibly a box of digestive biscuits. She didn't seem to mind because it wouldn't be long before a package arrived in the mail.

Grannie loved people; whenever she met them, she would include me in the conversation. When she was young, she and her brother, Godfrey, loved playing practical jokes, and she must have stirred things up among her family and friends. She was very fond of animals and was completely comfortable with them. She had grown up with all kinds of them at Benmore, the family home and farm.

My grandfather took a keen interest in everything I did and especially what I had been doing at school. I wonder if he might have been reliving his own years there. As a member of the clergy, he must have known so many people during his life and understood their pain and sorrow. We had good conversations, and I found them very helpful. When I had questions about what was happening at school that worried me, he seemed to understand. He made everything clearer and easier to face.

One day I was telling him about morale at the school and how it was affected by the example of the prefects; he told me of an experience he had when he was head prefect. Several boys were found drinking alcohol, which was strictly forbidden and likely to result in their expulsion. Their names were reported to the prefects who called the boys together and told them that they would have to report what they had done to the headmaster.

However, they also told the boys that if they each made a promise to obey all the school rules during their time there and never drink alcohol at school again, they would not give the headmaster their names. My grandfather said that when they reported the incident to the headmaster, but not the names, he commended them on their leadership and how they handled the situation and accepted their actions.

Grandad had a strong faith and great wisdom but didn't press it on people. He explained why a Christian faith could give one strength and ways we could practice it. Prayers were said with sincerity and were a daily practice. He had been a strong influence on many people. He encouraged me to see my Christian faith as essential to my character and behavior, and he played an important part in this through our many conversations. I learned from the examples and stories he told me about people, their experiences, and how they faced them.

He had a passion for outdoor games, especially golf and tennis but also croquet and ping pong. His favorite book was *Alice in Wonderland*, and often he would refer to passages relating them to real life situations that we would experience. After my grandfather finished his schooling at BCS, he went to St. John's College, Oxford, for his MA and was a member of the Oxford rowing team. An oar from his Oxford team's victory over Cambridge hangs in the summer cottage at Tadoussac. He was ordained in the Anglican church and married my grandmother, Caroline Anne Rhodes in 1887.

After serving at St. Matthews Church in Quebec, he became Dean at the Cathedral in 1899. Trinity Cathedral is the first Anglican cathedral outside the British Isles. King George III donated some of his religious objects to the Cathedral and a special pew was kept for him, although he never used it. In 1915, my grandfather, like his father, became the Anglican Bishop of Quebec.

He was a presence in the lives and minds of his congregation, including many who served in the Great War. I was told that after losing his eldest son in the war he spoke often of his desire for lasting peace. When he retired as Bishop of Quebec in 1934, I was away at school. I wanted to write to him, but I wondered what to say. I decided to congratulate him on his fiftieth anniversary; but on his retirement, I told him that I couldn't imagine anyone else taking his place as Bishop and that I was glad he was retiring because he will now be a lot freer, and it will take loads of responsibility off his shoulders and give him a chance to better enjoy the next twenty years or so. I said he could have kept on for another ten years and still be the best man in Canada for the job.

Each year I was at BCS, my grandfather would come to the school as Bishop of Quebec to confirm the boys in the annual Confirmation service, and I would see him then, of course.

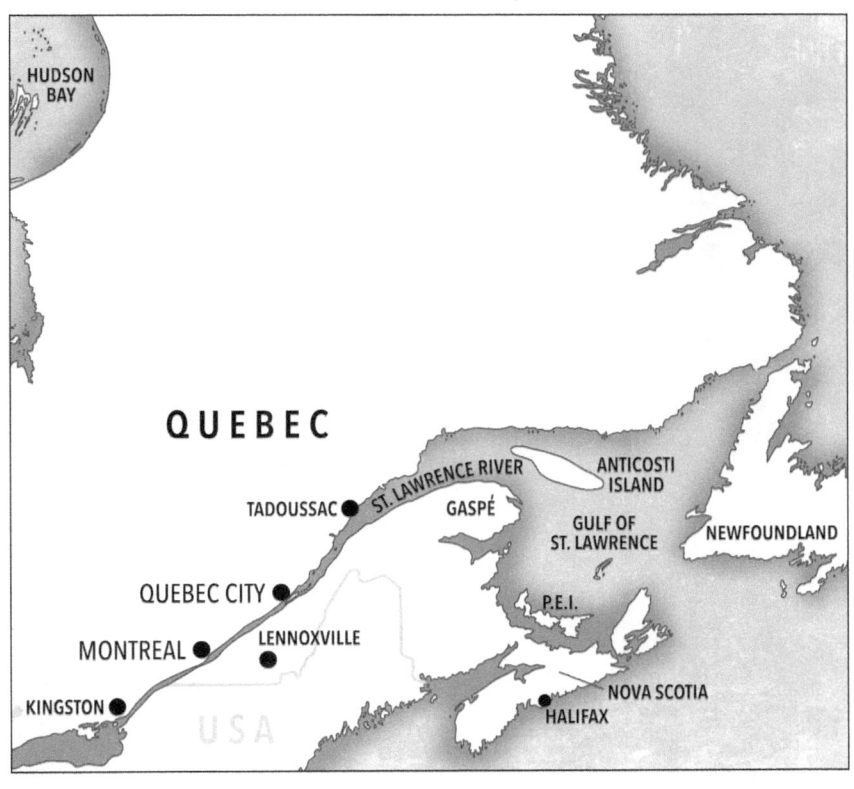

Jimmy and Jean on the lawn of Byrnhyfryd, Tadoussac, 1923.

Jimmy and his grandfather Lennox Williams salmon fishing, Quebec, c1930.

FIVE

SUMMERS

The BCS school year ended in June. I looked forward to being with my family again as, most years, I hadn't seen them for almost ten months. As soon as the holidays began, I would take the train to Quebec City to meet my mother, Jean, and Ronnie, who would arrive there from Winnipeg. We stayed in the city with my grandparents for a few days before leaving for Tadoussac to spend the summer at my grandparents' cottage.

The way to get to Tadoussac was by ship because roads beyond Quebec City were hardly passable among the hills on the north shore that rise almost directly from the river's edge. There are villages along the shore of the river, but the roads that connect them are rough, and people frequently get stuck. Almost all transportation to these villages was by water. A railway, built in 1919 from Quebec City, took you to Murray Bay and the Manoir Richelieu Hotel, but Tadoussac was fifty miles downriver over more mountains and worse roads. You also had to cross the Saguenay River. Getting to Tadoussac by ship was undoubtedly the way to go.

Canada Steamship Lines (CSL) had a regular service from Quebec to Tadoussac. Every summer, I went by ship, usually with my mother, sister, brother, and often one or more of my cousins. I was always excited about going there, but the anticipation of boarding the big white ship had me counting the days. When the time came, we would leave the city walls and descend to Lower

Town to the port beside the river. Although I had poor marks in history at school, I was well-versed in stories about Quebec. My grandfather told me of the many characters who came here and the reasons. Samuel de Champlain chose it as the capital of New France when he arrived in 1608.

He built the stone-walled fortress high above the St. Lawrence River and most of it remains today. I loved Quebec's deep-water port because it was usually filled with large ocean liners, warships and merchant vessels. It remains open in winter, a thousand miles inland from the Atlantic Ocean. Almost everything in the city is made of stone, its walls, gates, houses, churches, and the narrow streets of cobblestone. I could imagine being in old Europe or New France. The British captured Quebec from the French in 1759, and it was only sixteen years later that the Americans, led by Benedict Arnold, attempted to capture the city from the British. Much of the action occurred in the old port where we boarded the ship for Tadoussac. I learned about the American invasion of 1775 from my grandfather who was reading a book about Quebec by Willis Russell, written in 1867. It was called *How it was and How it is* and it told the story of Benedict Arnold leading a force from Maine up the Kennebec River to Lake Megantic and down the Chaudière River to capture the city.

Quebec was defended by General Guy Carleton's British garrison, including the Fraser Highlanders. I could visualize the attack because I knew exactly where it happened, on a very narrow street directly under the cliffs that rise to the city walls. At that time, the river came right up beside Sou-le-Cap, the narrow street where Arnold led his men. I could imagine what it had been like when, at the barricade on Sault-au-Matelot, Arnold was shot in the knee, and the British defeated the Americans. The streets in Lower Town, beside the port, cannot be much different today than they were in 1775, and we had to pass through them on our way to board the CSL ship.

Sou-le-Cap is so narrow I felt I was almost inside people's homes with the noise of banging pots, the smell of cooking, and the laundry hanging over the narrow street. Nearby was where Champlain made his first settlement while he built the city ramparts, and he began construction of the old stone church, Notre Dame des Victoires. Lower Town, next to the busy port, was a contrast to the walled city high above and was occupied by ships' chandlers, artisans, warehouses, merchant homes, and banks.

The CSL ship arrived in Quebec at 6 A.M. from Montreal. On the mornings we sailed, we would climb the gangplank to board shortly before 9 A.M. I hardly slept the night before; I was so excited. I would stand on the pier and look up at this beautiful white ship with its many decks and would wonder how it would feel to be its captain. When the ship pulled away from the dock onto the big river, we looked back at Quebec City, high on the rocks, brilliantly lit by the morning sun. It was a sight I will never forget.

Leaving Quebec, the ship sailed past Île d'Orléans and followed the St. Lawrence River as it flows northeast. We were all together on the boat most years; sometimes, our cousins were with us. There were games for the children, and we could watch horse races for the adults along the floor of the ballroom. Betting on them was pretty fun. The horses were 18 inches high, and most were named after winners of the Kentucky Derby. In 1934, when traveling alone, I bet on the winning horse called Cavalcade and won a dollar. On board the ship, you always met other people you knew. Most were my parents' or grandparents' friends, but many passengers were Americans taking the entire cruise or staying at the CSL hotels in Murray Bay or Tadoussac. In late morning, the ship passed Baie St. Paul and Isle aux Coudres, named after its hazelnuts in 1535 by Jacques Cartier.

Lunch was served in the ship's elegant dining room with its white tablecloths and waiters dressed in uniform. It was a full meal and ice cream was always available for dessert. While we were eating lunch the ship arrived in Murray Bay, and I was always fascinated by how the ship maneuvered into the dock. Sometimes, the tide and current made landings difficult, and the best part was watching the crew toss the lines to those on the pier. They frequently missed, which must have annoyed the captain who had hoped for a clean landing. The ship gave three blasts on its whistle to say "hello" and three more when we said "goodbye." As we cruised down the river in the afternoon, the orchestra played in the ballroom, where the adults gathered for tea. The next stop was St. Simeon, also on the river's north shore, where some passengers took the ferry across to Rivière du Loup on the south side. The ship was scheduled to arrive in Tadoussac at 5:30 P.M.

Three CSL ships sailed from Quebec to the Saguenay River: S.S. *Quebec*, S.S. *Tadoussac*, and the oldest, S.S. *Saguenay*, removed from service in 1931. They were all white and looked very similar, with their two red, white, and black funnels. They had luxurious cabins, some with bunks, but unfortunately, we never got to sleep in them because traveling from Quebec to Tadoussac was only a one-day trip.

Navigation on the St. Lawrence River is challenging. There are significant tidal changes, strong currents, frequent high winds, and often dense fog. Ocean-going traffic is heavy, and we would see freighters carrying goods to Europe or imports to Canada. If lucky, we might see an ocean liner carrying passengers, usually on the Liverpool to Montreal run. Everyone in Quebec City remembers what happened in 1914 when, in dense fog, the *Empress of Ireland* collided with a Norwegian freighter and sank in 14 minutes. This happened two hundred miles downriver from Quebec near Rimouski, and over 1,000 passengers drowned, more than the *Titanic's* loss two years earlier.

Most of the time I was on the CSL ships we had good weather. There was always so much to see. At the village wharfs we watched the smaller local boats, called *goelettes*, being loaded with goods to carry up and down the river, delivering them to local villages along the shore. They were the dominant mode of transport for lumber and other supplies. *Goelettes* were built of wood, designed over many generations to handle the choppy waters. Usually propelled by what sounded like an old truck engine, they sometimes were helped by a sail. They were family owned and operated, and a small cabin was mounted high on the stern where the family and crew lived. Laundry was usually hanging out to decorate their rigging.

The water in the St. Lawrence River is slightly green, most noticeable once the ship turns northwest toward the mouth of the Saguenay River and the bay at Tadoussac. Here, it passes by a red lightship marking a long reef and then crosses a clear line where the green of the St. Lawrence meets the deep blue of the Saguenay. The St. Lawrence River is twenty-five miles wide here, and we feel the brisk northwest wind coming down the Saguenay.

White spouts of water are forced upwards from the choppy rip tides and sparkle in the brilliant sun, a contrast with the clear blue sky and the deep blue water. Sometimes the white Arctic whales swam out to welcome us. It was a memorable moment, and my excitement grew more as the ship cruised into the large well-protected bay at Tadoussac and pulled alongside the wharf, where family and friends waved to greet us.

Tadoussac sits at the mouth of the Saguenay River, a deep-water fjord that flows into the St. Lawrence from Lac St. Jean, 100 miles to the northwest. It is tidal, salt water, and extremely deep, with high cliffs on each side. A beautiful bay with sandy beaches protects the village of Tadoussac. Rising behind the beach are cliffs where homes have been built over the years. From them, you can watch all the activities in the bay, including visits by the whales. For generations, people in Tadoussac have watched them as they surfaced and fed in the Bay. The most frequent and larger visitor is fondly named the "Grampus." This is a minke whale about 18 feet in length.

The pure white Arctic whales have remained year-round since the end of the Ice Age. They are curious and friendly and would come alongside us when we were out rowing in boats. The water is a very cold 48 degrees, but as children this never prevented us from playing on the sandy beach where the hot sand warms the water when the tide comes in. This is the north country, and you feel it immediately. The air is clean and clear. The scent of the northern woods and salt water mixed with cool sea air strikes you as a potent and healthy elixir. The trees of the spruce forests are of many shapes, sculpted by the strong winds and harsh winters. Summer days could be warm, but the evenings were cool. There is also rain, wind, and fog. Sometimes you heard the fog horns all night, and as you awoke in the morning, you listened, hoping they would stop, indicating that the fog was lifting. When the sun shone in the mornings, *les mouches noir*, the black flies, swarmed. This could be uncomfortable for those not accustomed to them, especially when camping or fishing, but the wind usually blows them away.

My great grandfather, Col. Rhodes, built his cottage in Tadoussac in 1860. He explained in a letter to his father in England that "during the summer we all move to where there are the pleasures and advantages of the seaside," and he described how his children made great use of the rivers and lakes around it with their boating, camping, fishing, and hunting. He must have wished that future generations of his family would enjoy their summers there too. Today, his descendants are surrounded by other families who built their own cottages to enjoy this summer community together. Rhodes's house was left to my grandmother, and I am the fourth generation to be there.

When considering Tadoussac's history, some would undoubtedly feel that most important was Samuel de Champlain's arrival in 1603 on his first voyage to the New World and his decision to establish it as a small and continuing settlement. The protected harbor provided a base where he could keep his ships while sending his smaller boats up the river to Quebec. His legacy in Canada is well known, especially for how he got along with the indigenous tribes. On his arrival in Tadoussac, there was a large gathering of the regional tribes just across the Saguenay River, on a point near today's village of Baie Sainte Catherine. We can see it from our house. Champlain went over to join them and began a friendly and supportive relationship that continued through his many years in New France.

I went to Tadoussac almost every summer. As young children, we played on the beach below my grandparents' house, building forts in the sand and trying in vain to stop the incoming tide. A steep winding path led from the home to the beach, and it was fun to run down, but it was a long climb back up. The water in the bay is icy but we didn't mind, and my grandmother and her friends would float in it happily almost daily. My family had several boats: a sturdy north shore canoe made of wood with two sets of oars, a lighter skiff, and the white boat, a larger and very safe craft that we thought must have once been a lifeboat for some ship. They were all moored off the beach, and we reached them by paddling out in a small rectangular punt. We loved rowing around in the boats, often imagining we were the CSL ships passing each other.

They also gave us access to sea creatures we could not get from the beach, such as starfish and sea urchins that clung to the sides of the wharf. A favorite was rowing across the Saguenay River for picnics, when we were required to have an adult with us. Our cousin, Billy Morewood, loved boats and picnics and she was always ready to be the adult with us. Our days were full of experiences, and during the evenings at home, we could tell the adults about them – but perhaps not all of them.

During the winter of 1931 the Rhodes house burned to the ground. It had been there for seventy-one years and had given the family many happy memories. A new house was built in the exact location, designed by our cousin, Frank Morewood, an architect. He was married to another cousin, Carrie Rhodes. Because of my grandparents, it became known as the Williams house, but local people still called it *Maison Rhodes*.

My grandfather, being of Welsh descent, gave it the name Brynhyfryd because of its beautiful view from high above the Bay. It was painted white and had a red roof. Like all the houses in Tadoussac, the walls were thin and made of spruce or pine, and you could hear through them easily. The wood floors were painted, often in different colors for different rooms. The cottages in Tadoussac were not winterized. There was a large wood stove in the kitchen for cooking and a stone fireplace in the living room that helped to keep us warm.

The fireplace at Brynhyfryd was made of large round stones found locally and rose to a very high ceiling above the second floor. Two pulpits protruded from the second-floor level on each side of the fireplace. I was never sure what these were for, but we used them to give sermons like we had seen our grandfather give at church. The bathrooms were modern, with a sink, bathtub, and toilet, and the white porcelain taps had bold black letters, "H" or "C" signifying hot or cold. But the letters were reversed, with the 'C' for cold on the left for hot water and the 'H' for cold on the right. We wondered if this was because the plumbers who installed them spoke French and thought 'C' meant *chaud*, the French word for hot. If so, what did they believe the 'H' stood for? There were no telephones except at the hotel, so when you wanted to talk to someone, you dropped by their house to see them. Electricity had recently been installed, and the candles and oil lanterns in most of the houses were replaced, except when the power went off. Food was stored in the icehouse for refrigeration, where large blocks of winter ice were placed deep in the ground and covered with sawdust.

When I arrived for the summer of 1934, I started playing

golf and tennis almost every day with aunts, uncles, cousins, and friends. A collection of tennis rackets hung on a rack in our house so anyone could play. The tennis courts were directly across the road and the rustic log clubhouse looked over the lower courts. Inside, a stone fireplace and a wood stove helped us to keep warm. Outside, the black flies were always ready to bite us.

Every Friday afternoon the community would gather, dressed in their whites, to sit on the porch, drink tea and watch the games on the two lower courts. There was quite a group about my age that included Ted Price, Jean Stockton, my sister Jean, my cousins, Betty Morewood, Phoebe and Ainslie Evans, and Elliot Turcot. After tennis or golf, we would often go for a swim in the lake behind the town. Dances were held on Saturday evenings at the Hotel. There was a good orchestra and sometimes we dressed up for a masquerade. The hotel was entertaining their guests, but they always made us feel welcome.

On Sundays we went to church. The local population, being of French origin, were Roman Catholic and attended a large and handsome stone church in the center of town. The English summer population were predominantly Protestant and went to the small Protestant Chapel that was built in 1866. The Chapel is beautiful, made of local wood and full of family memorials. Attending church on Sunday was expected and my grandfather conducted some of the services. I often think of him standing above us all in the beautifully carved pulpit. His sermons were brief.

I went to church at eight o'clock and again with Grannie at eleven. We were often late. She would tell me what it was like when she was a little girl. Her brothers sang in the choir and took up the collection, as my cousin Jackie and I sometimes did. We knew the hymns, and everyone sang in full voice. We wore our blazers, white flannel trousers, and school ties. Church was a time when all the families in the community came together.

My grandparents' house was always full of people. Aunts, uncles and my first cousins, Nan, Jackie and Michael Wallace usually were there along with my younger cousins, Joan and Susan Williams. We had such fun together. They loved playing golf and tennis and were always ready to go on picnics and run down the great sand dunes near Tadoussac. In the house, the parents tried to enforce discipline, but we still managed to stir up trouble and it was a very happy time for us all; moreover, I think our escapades succeeded in amusing our grandparents.

One time when my father was with us, and after days of no rain, he decided to take the hose from the garden and spray the dirt road to keep the dust down. When he had finished, he dropped the hose on the ground and went to turn off the water. Always ready for fun, Ronnie and my cousin Joan picked up the end of the hose and aimed the waterspout directly at him. He was not pleased, and in a loud voice, ordered them to stop. But they wouldn't let him get to the tap. Soon, a crowd gathered to watch. My father got very wet, and Joan and Ronnie, both aged six, had a wonderful time.

Guests almost always came to stay at our house. They were friends or relatives, and some returned every summer. I never knew how they were related to us, but they were ready to go on picnics, pick blueberries or play cards with us in the evenings. The house was always full and happy and there was a sense of order and routine. Each morning, before going to the dining room for breakfast, the entire family and guests would gather in the living room and kneel while Grandad said morning prayers. No one dared to be late or to miss prayers.

Mealtimes were strictly adhered to. A cook and maid from the local community prepared our meals. Breakfast was at eight o'clock with porridge, eggs and bacon, and milk from the local farmer's cow. Lunch at one o'clock was the main meal of the day. Supper was at six. We had to be on time for meals. The food was good and there was plenty. The dining room was large with one long table, but the younger children sat at a separate table from the adults. It was a big step when we were allowed to join the "grown-ups" table.

Grandad sat at one end, and we knew he could see everything we did. Mothers and aunts told us to keep our elbows off the table, sit straight, and finish everything on our plates. We were far from perfect, but I don't remember Grandad saying anything to scold us. He had his favorite salt and pepper shakers, called "Tweedle Dum" and "Tweedle Dee," from the poem in *Alice and Wonderland*.

Local produce in Tadoussac was limited. The growing season was short, so some of our vegetables and meat had to be brought by the CSL boat to Coté's grocery store. My grandfather brought live chickens from Quebec City so we could have chicken for every Sunday lunch. They lived in a coop just across the road in an empty field that belonged to the house. Every morning after breakfast, the children fed the chickens leftovers.

Spring lamb and fresh salmon were available locally and for frequent meals. The salmon was caught in large nets that ran out from the beach into the bay in front of our house. The cooks prepared a variety of sweet desserts. I remember the one called "squirrels' tails." After lunch, the adults would gather for tea or coffee, and instead of chocolate, we would be allowed one piece of *sucre la crème*, a French-Canadian sweet made from maple sugar.

My grandmother had grown up with a father and brothers who loved the woods and the water. During the family's early years in Tadoussac, they were often away on the lakes, rivers or in the woods. During the 1860s, Grannie's brothers, Army, Godfrey, William, Frank, and their friends, would row their boats up the Saguenay or down the St. Lawrence to camp and fish in the smaller rivers, often in very rough weather.

They thought nothing of being caught on the Marguerite or Bergeron rivers for a few wet nights because wind or fog prevented them from rowing their boats back home. Grannie told us that as teenagers, they were probably a threat to any living thing that could swim or fly and that they once found a bear cub, which they took home to Quebec. The boats were built to stand up to the difficult waters and had two sets of large oars. These are the same boats that are there today, refurbished or rebuilt.

During the next two generations, fishing and hunting played a lesser role and activities changed. By my generation, our morning outdoors began with golf or tennis. Most of us grew up on the nine-hole course just up the road from our house and we loved learning to play the game. On the wall outside the door to the dining room was a ladder of names ranked by the best score. The "ringer' score used your best score on each hole. The clubs we used were a rare collection of weapons with wood shafts and I was lucky to have a set of Bobby Jones irons, a three, five and a seven. The best hole on the golf course was number eight, a par four, and with a long drive you might make it over a deep gully to the green. When my grandfather's good friend, the Bishop of London, came to stay with us, I was asked to play golf with them. On the eighth tee, my grandfather offered a helpful comment that we often play safe and then hop the next shot over the gully to the green. As the Bishop of London addressed his ball, he said: "When the Bishop of London plays safe, God help the Church." He drove the green! Another time when he was in Tadoussac, I was included on a salmon fishing trip to the St. Jean River with my father, my grandfather, and the Bishop of London, who caught the only fish, a 24-lb. salmon. The bishop always dressed for dinner in his long purple cassock.

The arrival of the CSL ship at 5:30 P.M. each day was an important event. Meeting the boat was a popular activity, and the wharf was also a good place to meet others in Tadoussac. We wanted to see who was on the ship and were excited to welcome friends and relatives, especially if they were our age. The passengers walked up the gangway onto the wharf, followed by food and other supplies for the local shops.

The visiting tourists would take a horse-drawn *calèche* for a brief ride around the town before they reboarded the ship and continued up the Saguenay River overnight. When the boat returned the following morning, we might be at the wharf again, but this time, it was to say goodbye to someone leaving for home. What might have been a sad moment was filled with memories of happy times and the hope that we would see them again next summer.

When my father came to Tadoussac he had little interest in playing tennis or golf. He was more like my grandmother's generation and their passion for adventure and nature, and he preferred to head to the lakes and woods to camp or to fish on a river. He wanted to bring me along and I loved going with him. Sometimes my cousin Jackie would join us, but most often I was alone with my father. We caught lots of sea trout on the Saguenay, Marguerite and Bergeron Rivers and speckled trout in the lakes, always on a fly. I found the *Silver Doctor* and *Parmachene Belle* to be very successful with trout.

In 1935, my father was assigned a new posting in Saint John, New Brunswick. He was promoted to Brigadier and given command of Military District No. 7, which covered the Maritime Provinces. My parents moved to Rothesay, ten miles outside of Saint John. My mother and Ronnie went there in May, but Jean stayed in Winnipeg to finish her year at Rupertsland College. My father's new posting presented an opportunity that couldn't be passed up. He took me salmon fishing on the Restigouche River in New Brunswick, and we spent a few wonderful days at the Millionaires Pool. The fishing was excellent. I loved fly fishing and think I got pretty good at casting a salmon rod.

One evening, while staying up on the lakes to the north of Tadoussac, we watched the northern lights until after midnight. The sky was brilliant with vertical pipes of light reaching high in the dark northern sky. It was a spectacular sight. We fished for speckled trout in those lakes, and at other times we fished on the rivers at the Bergeronnes and Les Escoumins for sea trout. We walked up the rivers, wading in our shorts and shoes. On one of these trips, I caught so many sea trout I couldn't carry them, so I stuffed them in my pockets, but then promptly slipped and fell into the stream. Some of the fish floated away. We continued to fish until dark.

Those times away in the woods or on the lakes were very special. We had good chats, and I began to appreciate more what his life and career had been like and what being out in nature meant to him. In our conversations, rather than dictate his beliefs to me, he encouraged me to do things. He often offered examples of others. I sensed that significant things were happening in the larger world and Europe. He didn't go into detail, but I felt he was worried. While he was Commanding Officer in Montreal, he had to make many public speeches. He told me that once he was rapped over the knuckles by National Defense Headquarters for warning the public about the international situation in Europe and Japan. He referred to Headquarters as "the powers that preferred to keep their heads in the sand."

In early August, he received the telegram we had both been waiting for. It said:

SELECTED FOR ADMISSION RMC. STOP.
HE SHOULD REPORT TO COMMANDANT
RMC, KINGSTON, AT 2 P.M. STANDARD TIME
SATURDAY, AUGUST 31.

I was on my way to Royal Military College.

Jimmy and Ronald, 1936.

Royal Military College, Kingston, Ontario, 1938.

SIX

MILITARY COLLEGE

I reported to Royal Military College (RMC) in Kingston, Ontario, as a "gentleman cadet" to pursue an engineering degree in the class that would graduate in 1939. As with every cadet, I was given a number, and mine was 2432.

RMC has a role similar to that of the US Military Academy at West Point and the British Royal Military Academy at Sandhurst. Its stated purpose is to provide a complete education in all branches of military tactics, fortification, engineering, and general scientific knowledge in subjects connected with and necessary for a thorough knowledge of the military profession.

I was impressed that so many outstanding people had attended the College before me, yet I didn't know where this would lead me. I understood that I had to put every effort into making a success of my time there, and I knew my parents had high expectations for me to do well. They were not the only ones. Before arriving at RMC, I received a letter from my grandfather. He wished me well, writing:

> *You will enter upon a new phase of your life at RMC and if you 'play the game' and exert your full powers, mental and physical, I feel sure that you will be even more successful than you have been at school. You will, of course, have to face greater temptations as one of a crowd of young fellows, some*

of whom will be slackers, and worse, feel possibly attractive and amusing. They may go 'into the rough', but I am confident that you will 'keep your eye on the ball', 'drive straight' and make a 'good round'. Keep your rule of going to the Holy Communion regularly; it will help you greatly not to 'slice' from the fairway.

I was moved by his words. It was his way to always put you at ease as he offered advice or gave his view on something. It was typical of him, with his love of games and sports, he liked using golf to frame his message. I launched myself into the College with enthusiasm.

My classmates came from all parts of Canada. Some had attended private schools, but many were from public schools. Some came from England and there were others, like me, born in England, whose fathers had served in the War, but returned to Canada afterward. During the next four years I would get to know them very well.

We were called the "fourth class" in our first year because we had four years before graduating. We were treated as recruits and given many duties and tasks to perform. Any ideas we might have had about our importance were quickly removed. When crossing from one building to another, we couldn't just walk; we had to run everywhere, even while carrying our books. We were inspected daily on how we organized our gear. Our uniforms hung on hangers precisely one inch apart, and shoes in pairs were lined up perfectly. Life at RMC was demanding, disciplined, and directed toward building character.

The academics were challenging, and the curriculum was extensive and included regular college courses and military subjects. We were not trained to be soldiers, but we were given the rudiments of the profession of arms. The honor system was strongly emphasized, along with the value of discipline and the obligations of citizenship. The motto of RMC is *Truth, Duty, Valour*, and the principles of each were imbued in the way we were to treat those under us and those over us while also exhibiting sobriety and moral courage. We were introduced to *noblesse oblige*, a French term translated as "nobility obliges," meaning our position brings with it the duty to do the right thing for others.

RMC is located on Point Frederick, a peninsula on the St. Lawrence River with Kingston harbor to the west and Navy Bay to the east. The autumn and spring were beautiful, but the winter could be windy, damp and sometimes with heavy snowfalls. The College grounds were impressive, and in time I grew very proud of them. The Mackenzie building, built in 1876-78 with stone chimneys, a four-story tower and five bays on either side, is the centerpiece, and among other buildings formed the parade ground and playing fields.

On parade, we wore our uniforms, scarlet tunics, and a white helmet or pillbox. Inside the buildings, photographs of former cadets recognized for their courage and service hung on the walls. Each day at college was very full and I found it hard to meet the demands of my studies, sports, and the required drills and training. We were often exposed to events in the larger world outside, and visitors frequently came to speak about their experiences that were relevant to us.

On January 20, 1936, King George V died. He was regarded very highly and had been king since 1911 and during the Great War. The war had taken a toll on his health and his passing was felt with great sadness. The heir to the throne, the Prince of Wales, was very popular and became Edward VIII. However, this was not to last. The King is the head of the Church of England which does not approve of remarriage after divorce and Edward VIII insisted on marrying Wallis Simpson, an American divorcee. This led to a crisis. By December of that year, under pressure from England's Prime Minister, Stanley Baldwin, and from the many Dominions of the Empire, Edward decided to abdicate, the first British monarch to voluntarily resign from the job. Britain would get a new king, his brother Bertie, who became George VI.

That same winter, the 1936 Olympics were being held in Garmisch-Partenkirchen, Germany. Canada had sent 29 athletes and placed ninth in the overall medal count. What happened in hockey captured our attention because it was the first time Canada failed to win the gold medal. The Port Arthur Bearcats, representing Canada, finished second to a British team that included several Canadian players, causing a needless controversy. We were all aware that the games were contentious because of the antisemitic policies of Adolf Hitler and the Nazi Party. The year before, Jews in Germany had lost their citizenship.

Visiting teams at the Olympics were expected to give the Nazi "Heil Hitler" salute. We were pleased to learn that when the Canadian team paraded, smiling and dressed in their Olympic uniforms, they performed a similar salute, but with their arms outstretched to the side rather than to the front, as the Nazis did. They were performing the actual traditional Olympic salute. The difference was lost on the German crowd which erupted in cheers.

It took me a while to settle into my college subjects. I had good marks in mathematics, mechanics, and military engineering but difficulty with English and history. New courses were added in tactics, topography, civil engineering, physics, and military law, and I felt considerable stress from the workload. I wrote the Dominion Land Surveyor's exams along with twelve other cadets in January. The professors told me that it was valuable to pass these exams, but preparation involved a lot of extra classes and work. They were chiefly about "light" in physics, which was not covered in our usual courses. At the end of February, I received notice from the DLS Board of Examiners that my results had not been found satisfactory because I had failed two of the subjects. Despite this, my marks had improved by the end of my second year, and I came seventh in my class of fifty-three. I had become far more comfortable with the all-around nature of life at the college, which placed a high value on athletics, our studies, and training related to the military. I was a member of the rifle team, and I took on revolver training. I enjoyed horseback riding, and while some cadets had prior experience, I had the advantage of riding with my father when we lived in Winnipeg. The college training included jumping, with two jumps right after the other, fifteen feet in between, and riding with our arms folded and no stirrups. I came off frequently until I mastered it.

We progressed to doing more jumps, riding two and then three together and then in fives. It was fun. Our daily schedule was full, but we were encouraged to write letters and read. I wrote to my parents weekly and often to my grandparents and others in my family. Receiving letters was important to us because it gave us news of family, friends, and events at home and abroad.

My parents had always encouraged my sister and me to read books, and at college, I learned to enjoy Stevenson, Dickens, and poetry by Tennyson, Byron, Milton, and Shakespeare. In a letter to my parents, I told them that I had just read Sir Walter Scott's *Antiquity* and thought it was one of the best he had written.

Being at RMC meant that I was away from home, of course, but I was much more connected with my parents than when I was at BCS. They had moved to a new home, and I spent my holidays with them. My father had been appointed District Officer in Command (DOC) of District No. 4, headquartered in Montreal, and my parents had found a home in Montreal West. It was a short trip from Kingston by train, and I could get home easily to be with them. They were happy to be back in Montreal.

My sister Jean went to Trafalgar, a private school for girls, and Ronnie, now age five, went to a local public school. Perhaps most important was that my father and I could now share a common interest. I was fully engaged in RMC, and it was something my father knew well from his days as a member of its faculty. He also knew the world of the military and anyone of importance in it. He took an interest in world affairs and seemed aware and informed of what was happening. We found many subjects that we could talk about.

He stressed the need to put my all into my work, and sometimes, I felt he worried that I was not working hard enough. I would explain how difficult it was when there was so much diversion, with so many courses, sports, and other activities, and when the time to study comes, you feel so tired you want to relax. Of course, he was fully aware of this. I tried to explain how much I wanted to make good and that I was grateful for what he and my mother had done for me. "I don't want to just be another soldier who lives and dies as a Major or something. I want to do something useful." I knew that a soldier's life could be a good one, and in my letters, I said that I intended to make it so and would hate to let them down. I was also wondering if the Air Force would be the thing to go into by the time I graduated. I thought I might enjoy the feeling of being free–flying like a bird with such unlimited power of movement; or perhaps the tank corps, or the engineers would be the thing. I loved poetry and thought I might take it seriously. I told my parents I thought poetry is rather a life for men of mind, not of physical abilities, but that a poet does so much for mankind. He is doing good, and something everlasting. Poetry is immortal.

I didn't want to do something that would die with me. God must have put me here for a reason. I wondered what that was, and what I was best suited to do with my life – certainly not in business, more likely as a soldier; but how, where, and when? My mind was full of thoughts like these. When I wrote about them to my parents, I didn't forget to ask my mother to send me some George Washington instant coffee and powdered milk to help me stay awake and study.

The term following Christmas is a long one. Twice during

my years at RMC, the College was honored by a visit from the Governor General of Canada, Lord Tweedsmuir, to deliver a lecture. As Commander in Chief, he represents the King as sovereign of Canada. He was sometimes known as John Buchan, from Scotland, who had become an accomplished author of many good novels such as *Prester John* and *Thirty-nine Steps*.

He also wrote a biography of Oliver Cromwell which was the subject of his first lecture. Because my father knew him, I wrote to say that I found it very interesting, but because he read the lecture, I thought that it lost some of its strength and that it might have been easier and more efficient for me to read it on my own. Two years later he returned to speak about his close friend, T. E. Lawrence of Arabia, and I found what he told us to be both valuable and compelling. He described how, during the Great War, Lawrence had inspired the Arab revolt in the Hejaz to free the Arabs from Turkish rule and welcome an independent Arab nation while assisting the British campaign in Palestine against the Ottomans. He recommended Lawrence's book, *Seven Pillars of Wisdom*, which I had read because I received it as a prize at BCS. At age twenty-six, Lawrence entered the intelligence branch of the army as an Oxford-educated archeologist with no military training. He had learned to speak Arabic and understood and embraced Arab culture completely.

Dressed in his robes, and dagger, he led the Arab tribes as an army that paralyzed the left wing of the Turkish forces fighting the British. It was an interesting story but what I remember most was how Lord Tweedsmuir explained strategy and tactics as the two main branches of military science. He pointed out that, while tactics are constantly changing with the discovery of new weapons, the principles of strategy are permanent because the object is to win by weakening your enemy's will to resist. Lawrence, acting almost independently of British forces, managed to bring together diverse Arab tribes that frequently fought each other, into an armed force. His critical strategy was to attack and destroy the railway the Turks had built to control Arabia.

He succeeded in defeating and removing the Turks while offering the Arabs control of their land. What we know as tactics today is only a remote relation to what they were in the past. Strategy is about striking at the enemy's nerve center and in modern war not only the armies and navies, but the whole strength of a nation is drawn into the conflict. To win, you must persuade your enemy that it's not worthwhile for him to go on. I thought about this afterwards and wondered how the Army and Navy would play a strategic role in the future. Could the Air Force become a strategic offensive force by bombing enemy ships, armies, and factories and weakening their ability to resist? New aircraft were being developed that might be capable of this.

Spring came and we began to move outside for sports and other activities, including an active track and field competition. My chance to enjoy this was suddenly interrupted by pains in my stomach. They were diagnosed as appendicitis, and I went into the Kingston General Hospital for surgery. They kept me there for 12 days. This prevented me from doing any physical activity for a time, but fortunately, it happened after the hockey season was over. I didn't make the senior hockey team that year. It was limited to twelve players, but I felt confident I could make it next year and play on it for my last two years at RMC. It was my favorite sport. We followed the Stanley Cup playoffs, and each had our favorite team. That season, the Canadiens went from last to first place in the Canadian Division. Howie Morenz returned to the team, but in February a tragic injury led to a blood clot in his leg, and he died. It was a huge loss to the hockey world, and many mourned his death. Howie Morenz had joined the Canadiens in 1924, when

Sprague Cleghorn was the captain and star defenseman, and they won the Stanley Cup for the first time. Morenz scored a hat trick and the winning goal. The Canadiens did not win the Stanley Cup in 1937.

On May 12, 1937, the College celebrated the coronation of King George VI and Queen Elizabeth. Edward VIII, his elder brother who had abdicated in December, was now called the Duke of Windsor. It was a very joyous time for us all and I found the ceremony and its traditions filled me with emotion and pride in the British Empire. The coronation was held in Westminster Abbey in London and celebrated throughout Canada and the Empire. The Royal Princesses, Elizabeth and Margaret, were part of the procession and ceremony.

When my second year at RMC ended, I attended an artillery training camp in Petawawa, Ontario, during the summer. I was attached to the 5th Field Battery as a Section Commander. My father suggested that I consider artillery as one of my future options. I had no previous artillery training, and I enjoyed the camp. I decided to take the RCHA (Royal Canadian Horse Artillery) commission for the whole summer next year.

When I returned to RMC to begin my third year, I was thinking more seriously about my future and looking at my career choices. I can't recall when I became aware that there might be another war. I had grown up in a family where war had been a reality. In his army career, my father was dedicated to the nation's defense, and he was well-informed about what was happening in the world and how Canada might be affected. His concern for Europe and the warnings about Hitler and Germany by people like Winston Churchill were different than the intelligence experts from the governments of the British Commonwealth, the USA, and France, who, he said, did not appear to be very worried. Whatever Britain might face in Europe, it would undoubtedly involve Canada. I accepted that for my generation, whatever career we chose, we had a responsibility to our country and its defense.

I was pretty certain now that I wanted to pursue a career in the armed forces, and the idea of the Air Force had become more interesting. Aviation was making significant advances: Trans Canada Airlines (TCA) announced that it was linking to international flights, connecting to Britain and Australia. TCA had been formed the previous year with its first flight between Vancouver and Seattle using a Lockheed Model 14 aircraft. I was interested in flying, but I had yet to fly in an airplane. While a career in the Air Force had increasing appeal, what would I do when I finished RMC in June 1939?

When I asked my father about the Air Force, he responded positively but admitted he was of the "old school." He looked upon the RAF as a new arrival among the services, without the traditions or type of officer found in the Army. However, he told me that a future war would be different. Aircraft had played a minimal part in the Great War. There were dog fights and heroes, but he thought new airplanes and engines would enable them to play a more significant part. I remembered Lord Tweedsmuir's talk on tactics and strategy and wondered if advances in aircraft might make them part of a future strategic offensive.

I decided that I needed to know more about my choices, and when I gathered some information, I wrote to my father and asked about his views. I learned about a career path in the British Army, including the pay, promotions, and leave. I would earn $2.50 a day and $3.50 a day after seven years. I could be posted in the Infantry somewhere in the United Kingdom, Northern Ireland, the Mediterranean, Palestine, Egypt, Sudan, India, Burma, Malaya, or China, returning after five years. I would be expected to pay for my uniforms, obtain permission to marry, and receive a marriage allowance, but only after age thirty. So much for the Infantry and the Artillery, which I dismissed because of what seemed a long and unpredictable course to advancement.

I had more interest in the Air Force. I found that the pay was better as a pilot officer in the RAF (Royal Air Force) and told my father. The RCAF (Royal Canadian Air Force) did not have an officer training program. As a graduate of RMC, to join the RAF I would have to take ten months of flight training at Camp Borden and at Trenton, Ontario to obtain my wings. After this I would report to the RAF in England and take two months of further training to achieve proficiency on the types of aircraft being used. I would then be assigned to a unit in England. As a pilot officer, I must pass the exams, and after four years I would be eligible for promotion to Flight Lieutenant.

I knew that the Royal Air Force was considered junior to the Royal Navy and the Army. It was officially formed in 1918 from the Royal Flying Corps and was organized only in the 1920s. I wondered about its future. Not only were new aircraft being developed, along with better weapons and bombs they would carry, but wouldn't the Army need aircraft for protection, intelligence and attacking the enemy? In a letter to my father, I asked him:

> *What do you think of this, Dad? My classmate, Mike MacBrien, tells me that for the RCAF, the course at Trenton is only six months, from 28 June to 20 December, with three weeks Christmas leave, followed by serving the rest of the 10 months as a pilot officer in the Canadian Air Force. Do you think it worth missing a year's seniority by going into the Air Force instead of the Infantry? And, of course, there is a certain element of danger in the Air Force, but conditions in wartime are a lot better. Can you get anywhere in the Air Force, I mean, have you any chance for high command or that sort of thing and could you go to the Staff College? If I was to go into the Air Force, I would have to take mechanical engineering, and I don't know whether I would enjoy it. I would like to go up in an aircraft sometime, just to see if I could stand the*

air and height. I suppose I could do that this coming summer couldn't I? Let me know what you think about the RAF.

After looking at all the details of pay, seniority, geography and promotion for each of the services I realized that this wasn't what should be most important to me. My father was a wartime and career soldier and naturally believed that there was value in the established Army and its traditions compared with a newly formed and more "junior" Air Force. I listened to him and respected his opinions, but in my search for information about a career in the forces, I may have been preoccupied with comparing the form and details of each rather than their importance in the future. Wouldn't I want a career in the force that was growing more significant in our country's future? I wasn't sure, of course, but I was beginning to have more than an intuitive feeling that the Air Force would be the one.

My father felt quite strongly that if I intended to make the Air Force my career I should apply as an officer in the RAF permanent force. The RCAF, although it had a very good history and its pilots had distinguished themselves during the Great War, it did not yet have the same degree of scope, number of aircraft and opportunities for a career officer that I might find in the RAF.

I was now several months into my third year, and I was finding it difficult. I had not started well, and I failed chemistry on my exams. At Christmas, I came home to spend the holidays with my parents in Montreal. It was nice to be with them, but it was also a busy time for them. That autumn, during the debutante season in Montreal, Jean "came out" and was presented. Because of this, she was attending many parties and balls. I knew her so well and I wondered if she enjoyed it all. Considering my father's position in Montreal, my parents probably felt it was the right thing for Jean to do. I was far too involved in my life at RMC to participate in the many social events and I returned to the College at the beginning of the year and the start of the hockey season.

Sports were an essential part of college life, and there was a great selection of choices. In boxing, I won the middleweight championship and the officers' Long Course Cup. I also got involved in dinghy sailing, and we raced against McGill and qualified for the championships in Toronto. I played on the rugby team against Ottawa College, Queen's University, McGill and the Trenton Flyers.

I loved all the team sports, but hockey was my favorite. I was on the RMC first team in both my third and fourth years and was fortunate to play defense with Mike MacBrien. We had become good friends, and Mike was a great example of team playing and leadership, always encouraging and supporting others who played with him. He made me appreciate the game so much more and I learned how a caring and good working team can make a difference. This is especially true in hockey but also in any team activity. We played against other colleges in the Ontario Hockey Association, but the highlight of the season was the annual hockey match against the United States Military Academy at Westpoint.

In my third year the West Point game was held on March 5 at the conclusion of our hockey season. I had become a full member of the RMC team and was playing defense. The game this year was at West Point and our team of fifteen players traveled by bus to Montreal. We had enough time for dinner before boarding the overnight train bound for the USA, and I was able to see my parents at home. Our sleeping car was so hot that I doubt any of us slept. We got up about eight and had breakfast on the train before we arrived at West Point. At the station, we were met by our hosts, the cadets on the West Point team, and a collection of press-cameramen who followed our every move with their cameras and flash bulbs. We went up to the College by bus and were taken to our respective rooms. We paired off according to the positions we played on our team. For example, the West Point goalie was host for the RMC goalie; the center on the West Point team took the center of the RMC team under his wing and so on.

Each West Pointer became the special host for an RMC gentleman cadet, his opponent on the team. During our visit, these pairs became inseparable. My opposing defense player escorted me to his quarters, where I was assigned a bed and the locker of his obliging roommate, who had vacated for the occasion. At 11:00, we went to the rink for a half-hour practice. It was an extraordinarily large sheet of ice, much bigger than the Forum in Montreal.

We returned and went to lunch with the rest of the college. I was sitting in "L" Company. I think they go to "M" leaving out "J." It was an awfully nice mess hall shaped like a dog's leg. They had a parade for inspection after lunch, during which each of us inspected a company. I naturally inspected the "L" Company, and it was pretty interesting. Then five of them took me around the College and we saw a polo game between West Point and Cornell at their indoor Polo arena.

They also have an outdoor one and three riding schools. After this, we watched a West Point and Temple University gymnastics match. It was excellent gymnastics—I had never seen anything like it. We had enough time to see the end of a swimming and diving meet in their pool. At 5 P.M., they had tea, and afterward, I lay down for an hour before we went to the arena to play the game.

The game began with the playing of both national anthems, *God Save the King* and *The Star-Spangled Banner*. The traditions of the two colleges were followed at each match every year, whether the game was held at West Point or at RMC. Unlike many colleges, neither West Point nor RMC extended leaves of absence to cadets who may have wanted to accompany and support their team on its "out of town" trip. Consequently, while playing at West Point, the only cheering section which might be able to cheer along the RMC visiting team with Canadian songs, cheers, yells, and other vocal forms of encouragement, would have been our own players on our bench. Both modesty and practical considerations imposed the rule of silence on us. To remedy this unhappy situation, the West Point hosts divided themselves into two equal groups several days before the game; one group was designated to root for the home team according to its custom and practice, and the second

Jimmy in RMC hockey, 1939.

group was delegated to root for the visiting team. This was carried out with military proficiency and zeal. This second group rehearsed the songs and yells of Royal Military College to become a capable band of welcome ringers. They made it a point of honor to make even more and better noise than the band of West Pointers across the rink. The same procedure is followed when the game is played in Kingston, but in reverse.

It was a very close game. I got a cheer once when I bounced Harltins, a big boy playing defense who is also the center on their Rugby team and apparently runner up for an All-American center. However, he wasn't a great skater. RMC won the game 1-0, but West Point had a strong team. Afterwards, I saw Iso and Guy Smith, who I knew from summers in Tadoussac. They came to watch the game, and I was able to talk to them for a while. Guy was an RMC graduate and was in Canada's diplomatic service with the Trade Commission in New York. Iso was Ted Price's older sister.

It was about eleven o'clock when the game finished, and we went up to a dance in the gym for about three-quarters of an hour. It stopped at midnight, so we were not there for long. We all grabbed a girl and went cruising around to various night clubs in the town. The West Point chaps couldn't come out. I got back to bed at about six. It hadn't started to get light yet. The next morning, we didn't go to the breakfast parade, but at 10:30, we went on Church Parade. The chapel was beautiful, with a wonderful organ, and I saw Iso and Guy Smith again. After Chapel, the cadets took us to the Thayer Inn for a buffet lunch before we said goodbye to our wonderful hosts and boarded our bus for New York City.

When we were about to cross the beautiful George Washington Memorial suspension bridge, an announcer came on board to show us "little old New York." He was quite put out when we didn't want to stop to see Grant's Tomb. He had a real line telling us about New York, which he knew by heart, but he didn't get much response from us. Everything he showed us, he talked of in terms of money, a queer perspective on things. I knew that I didn't want to live in New York. We went everywhere, from Wall Street to the worst slums. They were pretty horrible. We briefly stopped at the Jack Dempsey Bar on 33rd Street on our way to dinner. Dinner was at the Paradise Club restaurant in Times Square, where ex-cadets of RMC were our hosts. It had a very good floor show, a bit crude in parts, and when it was over, we went to Radio City, where we just had time to see the Vaudeville show. I've never seen anything quite so huge as Radio City inside. After that, we walked to Grand Central Station, which took us a little time as we got a bit lost on the streets of New York. Our train left at 11:30 P.M., and when we arrived in Montreal the next morning, I had time to telephone my parents before boarding the train for Kingston.

It was customary for members of both teams to trade clothing and other college items with members of the other team. This gave us all something fun to bring home. We left on the trip with all kinds of items to trade. When the time came, I got one of their heavy dressing gowns for three gym vests and one of their light dressing gowns for a tie. I didn't think that was fair, so I gave the chap a swagger stick, too. Then I got one of their West Point sweater coats (brand new) for an old one of mine. It's really a lovely sweater coat. I also got a new set of pajamas for a belt. There were no startling bargains but only because no one wanted to cheat. They were so wonderfully decent to us. I brought a carton of cigarettes back, which the customs officer allowed, and I sold it for $2.00.

At the end of the 1938 season, Michael MacBrien was elected Captain of the first hockey team for next year. Before coming to RMC, Mike had played hockey and football at Ashbury College in Ottawa. He was an all-around athlete and set an example of good sportsmanship. Our fathers knew each other, had served in the war and became Major Generals, and like me, Mike was born in England. Our years of hockey, playing together as defensemen, were busy ones. We played against McGill, Loyola, Université de

Montréal, Bishop's, and Queens. The annual West Point game our last year was played at RMC. It was a close score of 4-3 and the first time that West Point won during the sixteen years that the series had been held. Although we were disappointed, we had a good feeling that our worthy opponent had at last won a victory, and the visiting West Point cadets were treated to the usual festivities, given a cheering section at the game and taken to the dance afterwards. A few weeks later, two members of the West Point team returned to RMC to present a trophy emblematic of the friendly sports rivalry and feeling of international respect between our two countries. This year's Stanley Cup also was played between our two countries. Toronto Maple Leafs and Boston Bruins were in the finals with Boston winning the series 4-1.

I finished my third year at RMC and came seventh in my class. I was disappointed as I had hoped for better. When we gathered to watch the graduating class ceremonies, the reality struck me that next year it would be my turn. I wanted so much to do better and to achieve something that would make my parents proud of me. I realized that I would have to work harder and be more effective in using my time. It was announced that Mike MacBrien would be our Battalion Sergeant Major for our final year. I felt he was the best choice from our class, a good leader, a team player, and a very nice person. I was very pleased for him. At the graduation ceremony, the Minister of National Defense, Hon. Ian Mackenzie, was the honored guest. In his remarks, he referred to a series of international crises that had implications for national security and said, "Each of you is given the trust and responsibility to serve your country. I wish you the best in the future that your country may be able to give. Keep rendering service to Canada, the Empire, and your fellow man."

Military College

During my years at RMC, I was able to be in Tadoussac for part of the summers. While I didn't realize it then, something happened during the summer of 1936 that would change my life. One afternoon at about 5:30, I was at the wharf with my usual group of friends. We had come to meet the CSL ship that was steaming into the bay to see who might be arriving in Tadoussac. When the ship was securely tied up to the wharf, the crew began to unload freight and produce for Coté's grocery store along with passenger luggage. The arriving passengers followed, walking slowly up the gangplank, which was steeper than usual because of the low tide. Ted Price and I were standing together when we noticed two attractive girls walking up the gangway. Ted, with his usual happy laugh, said to me. "You take that one; I'll take the other." Barbara and Mary Hampson were arriving with their parents to stay at the Hotel. It was their first time in Tadoussac, and it didn't take any time before they were welcomed to our group of friends. They had spent previous summers in Murray Bay, where their parents rented a house to get away from the summer heat in Montreal. It wasn't long before I got to know Barbara and began to call her Bar. We seemed to enjoy many of the same things and doing them together, and as the summer came to an end, I was surprised how downhearted I felt. When would I see her again? That September, when I returned to RMC, she left for England for the 1936-37 school year. She wrote letters to me and told me how much she was enjoying England and being at her school in Marlow on the Thames, just outside London. She went to Switzerland over the holidays and wrote about the wonderful skiing she was doing.

The following summer, when Bar returned to Tadoussac I was excited to see her again, and we spent much more time together. She was very popular, always fun, ready to take part in anything, and made friends easily. Bar was also game for surprises and always came up with creative ideas about what we could do. She was good at sports and loved to play golf, but tennis was her favorite. When we played against each other, she would usually win. Maybe one of those times when I lost, I realized I was in love with her.

We had such a fun summer with all our gang, going on picnics to the sand dunes at Moulin Baude, where we would run down the dunes to the beach below and meet on the rocks for a swim and lunch. Nearer Tadoussac there are many trails for walks and hikes. One that we enjoyed, was to walk along the beach to Pointe Rouge, climb up to the fairy circle, which was one of Bar's favorite spots, and return home through Languedoc Park and the woods. Bar had a sharp eye for four-leaf clovers, which were supposed to bring good luck. Whenever we saw a spread of clover on a lawn, they were all three-leaf, of course; except that somehow, Bar could pick out one or two four-leaf clovers from the thousands of others. She loved to sing and one of her favorite songs was "I'm looking over a four-leaf clover." She was always trying to get others to sing with her, which was a good thing because, although she looked beautiful when she sang, she couldn't hold a tune very well.

The summer of 1937, tragedy struck our family. On July 30, my grandmother, Nan Williams, died suddenly when we were all staying at her house in Tadoussac. She had always been active, and that day, she made her usual visit to the beach below, where she swam in the icy and refreshing water of the bay. She had returned, climbing the steep bank to the house, and began to feel ill. Her heart gave out at age seventy-six. It was devastating for all of us. I had not experienced a death in our family, and I felt especially close to her. She had a strong character and clear sense of right and wrong, but she loved to laugh and enjoyed mischief. I cherish the times I had with her. She was so good to me when I was at BCS, and earlier that summer, she had finished knitting a lovely, white, cable-stitched sweater for me with the RMC red stripes on its "v" neck. It was fortunate that, two months before she died, she was able to welcome her tenth grandchild into the world. Sheila Williams was born on June 4, a little sister for my first cousins, Joan, Susan and Jimmy. I was so pleased when her parents, my Uncle Syd and Aunt Enid, asked me to be her Godfather.

When the summer ended, and before I returned to RMC, I stayed in Montreal with my parents for a short time. Bar lived in Montreal, and I could see her for a few days. Her parents, Greville and Winnifred Hampson had a farm at Ste. Thérèse about twenty miles north of the city, where they raised prize Shorthorn cattle. Bar often went to the farm, but she also enjoyed her friends and often stayed in the city to be with them. She was pretty independent. On one occasion, she and her friends went off to New York City without telling her parents. She and her sister did lots together and had many friends in common. Mary was two years older. Bar was also very fond of her younger brother, John. After Bar returned from school in England, she continued her interest in painting and took art classes in Montreal. I saw a recent one she did of

Barbara Hampson on the wharf at Tadoussac, 1937.

Ferdinand the bull sitting peacefully in the pasture until he was stung by a bee. She loves stories of animals.

At Christmas that year, I saw Bar again, and we were able to go north to the Laurentian mountains to spend a few days skiing. We boarded the "ski train" from the city to the ski country. Along the way, it stopped at towns where skiers could get off at Shawbridge, Piedmont, Saint Sauveur, Mont Rolland, or Ste. Adèle, and ski southward on the trails before reboarding the afternoon train back to the city. Bar and I had a wonderful time skiing together at the Chantecler Hotel in Ste. Adèle.

In the summer of 1938, when we returned to Tadoussac, Bar and I were pretty serious about each other. I was very much in love with her, and the funny thing was that she seemed to love me. The year before, she had come up to Kingston for the RMC Christmas dance, and as always, there were a lot of people there. Bar was excited to see girls she knew from Montreal and others from Ottawa, where she had attended Elmwood, a girls' boarding school. She also knew a few of my classmates, Ted Price and Hugh Morrisey, and met others, including Mike MacBrien, and she joined into everything easily. When she came to the June 1938 ball at the end of my third year, her excitement was obvious. "I love coming to RMC. The dances are more fun than any I can remember, and I almost feel at home at the College."

That summer, Bar and I saw a lot of each other. When my father arrived in Tadoussac, we all went fishing together. It was the last time that we were all there together before the war. Ronnie was eight, Jean was nineteen and I was twenty.

When I returned to RMC for my final year in September 1938, our Commandant, Brigadier H. H. Matthews, was leaving the College. He had overseen many changes to the educational system, including adding a hospital, a new mess, a new gymnasium, and a wing on the Fort Frederick dormitory. Everyone wished him well. Our new Commandant, Brigadier HDG Crerar, DSO, had served in the war, led his battery at Vimy Ridge, and was awarded the DSO. He was also a graduate of RMC.

I was now committed to mechanical engineering because I intended to join the Air Force. I took the basic courses of Imperial and International Affairs, Military History, Tactics, Shopwork and Special Arms, and The History of the Air Force. Additional mechanical engineering courses included electrical, hydraulics, machine details, mathematics, mechanics and machines, thermodynamics, survey, and structural design.

I wanted to learn more about the RAF and how it was organized as an official service after the war ended in1918. Although the German bombing of England during the war was limited, it demonstrated the potential of an offensive bombing strategy for destroying an enemy's industrial and military infrastructure. It was believed that the bomber would always get through on its attacks, however an effective system of air defense would also be necessary.

My marks at the end of the autumn term were good and my report described me as "a conscientious, energetic and satisfactory platoon Commander." I was feeling more confident now about my future and the choice I was about to make. I would be graduating in six months and while the years had flown by, I felt I had traveled a long road through the courses, sports and other experiences at the College, I had learned so much from them, but I felt my capacity to understand, think and decide had also grown. I was ready to move on.

The traditional RMC Christmas dance was held on December 16. Bar was able to come up to Kingston to be there with me and my dance card was full of dances with her. It was a very happy time with seasonal decorations of holly and fir. Bar spent Christmas in Montreal with her parents, her sister and brother at their home on

McGregor Street, just across from where she and Jean had gone to Trafalgar School. I was disappointed that I would not be there to enjoy the holiday with her, but my parents had moved to Toronto, and I would be with them.

My father had been given command of Military District No. 2 in Toronto in December 1938. It was an important change for him in his career. Montreal had its challenges, and sometimes, my father spoke about the corruption in the city and its mayor, Camillien Houde. However, they had many good friends and enjoyed living there. Also, it meant they were close to my grandfather, who, after my grandmother died, had moved from Quebec City to live with my Aunt Mary and Uncle Jack Wallace in Montreal. My parents were quite sorry to leave Montreal.

I went to Toronto for Christmas, but it was a very short break. My parents' new home was in Rosedale, a nice residential area, at 45 Highland Avenue. My mother was happy with the garden and Ronnie went to Crescent school. On New Year's Day, my father brought me to a reception given by the Lieut. Governor of Ontario, Albert Matthews, and I wore my RMC uniform as a Gentleman Cadet Sgt. I knew that my father was proud of me. Knowing this spurred me on to finishing well at RMC and to preparing for what I would have to do after.

On January 3, I reported back to RMC and completed my application to the Royal Air Force. To be accepted for a permanent commission in the RAF, a candidate must be recommended by the Governor General of Canada on the report of the Commandant of RMC. I would have to be a provisional Pilot Officer after completing training and graduating with wings with the RCAF. Candidates were required to be British subjects, under twenty-five, unmarried, and medically fit. If accepted, I would become a Pilot Officer in the RAF Permanent Force. Within eighteen months of entry, I would have to pass examinations for promotion to Flying Officer. In January, my father helped with the application process by writing to the RMC Commandant, Brig, H.D.G. Crerar asking for his assistance with my records. The final training, prior to taking up a commission in England, seemed very complicated. I discovered that I would need to attend a flying school for three months, then go to Camp Borden for further training, and finally to Trenton, Ontario, where I would hopefully get my wings. My father might have preferred that I go into the Royal Artillery, but I was intent on joining the Air Force. A few months later, on May 4, the RMC Commandant received a telegram from the RAF Chief of Air Staff confirming that:

J.O. ALEXANDER SELECTED FOR ADMISSION TO FLYING TRAINING TO FILL VACANCY FOR APPOINTMENT PERMANENT COMMISSION GENERAL DUTIES BRANCH ROYAL AIR FORCE, SUBJECT TO GRADUATION AND PASSING X-RAY EXAMINATION.

I was thrilled when Brigadier Crerar gave me the news. This meant that my seniority would be dated from the date of my graduation from RMC, although I would have to do my training with RCAF and graduate with my wings in Canada before reporting in England.

In the spring and early summer of 1939, King George VI and Queen Elizabeth made a month-long tour of Canada, visiting every province. They also made a state visit to Washington D.C. where they met with President and Mrs. Roosevelt. On Sunday, May 21, they came to RMC, the first time a reigning monarch had visited the College. At about 8:40 P.M. their Majesties drove slowly onto the Parade Square, where our Cadet Battalion was fully drawn up in our full-dress, redcoat uniforms, and white helmets.

It was twilight as His Majesty got out of the car and began to inspect the RMC battalion of two hundred cadets. Each of us felt honored and happy, aware that it was an unparalleled circumstance for His Majesty to make an inspection of this kind. As their Majesties moved off the Square, passing in front of the Cadet Battalion, they were given the Royal Salute. Helmets were doffed and three cheers, both rousing and heartfelt, resounded from all of us. In response, the King raised his hat, and the Queen waved her hand as they drove off. I was a company sergeant, and it was a truly great experience for me to be there.

It was the King's great grandmother, Queen Victoria who confirmed the title of "Royal" on the College. When their Majesties first arrived at Quebec on the *Empress of Australia*, my grandfather, in his role as Bishop of Quebec, attended the state dinner. When they came to Toronto, my father and mother were both involved in the royal visit. Being in command of the Ontario District, my father had 10,000 troops on parade lining the streets as their Majesties drove to the Legislative Buildings. On another occasion during the visit, while the King was meeting with others, my father accompanied the Queen, motoring through downtown Toronto in an open car. He was fully dressed in his scarlet uniform and was mistaken for the King by some of the crowd and heartily cheered. The next morning, Toronto's newspaper, the *Mail and Empire* included a photograph of the Queen and my father, wrongly describing him as the King.

Ronald Alexander accompanying Queen Elizabeth,
Royal Visit to Canada, 1939

Our graduation ceremonies were held a few weeks later in June. It is hard to describe the emotion one felt. We had come together from many places and had passed the tests that so many before us had done since RMC was founded. My classmates came from all parts of Canada; nine were from Britain and one was from Hong Kong. I had made such good friends among them. Now they were heading off in different directions. "Pip" Nation, captain of the soccer team, was returning to England; Ken Ward had spent his summers with the navy and was probably headed there again; Chou Price would continue playing practical jokes and making people laugh wherever he went; Hugh Morrisey, who was called "Mickey" for impersonating Walt Disney characters, was headed for England. His sister was a good friend of Bar's. "Ike" Buchanan, an outstanding athlete, was headed to the Artillery; and my old friend Ted Price joined the Royal Canadian Regiment. Among them all, Mike MacBrien had been my closest friend during my years at the College. Mike was joining the Royal Canadian Air Force (RCAF) and since he had specialized in mining during his final year, I felt sure that in his future he would be flying over mining country. Of our class, twenty-three of us had already taken commissions in the permanent or regular Army or Air Forces.

Three had applied for commissions in the Royal Canadian Navy. Every member of our class received a silver dinner gong with a miniature swagger stick hanging on its side. The gong displayed the RMC crest and included everyone's signature and their cadet numbers. It was a wonderful reminder of who we had shared the RMC experience with; and when struck, it made a resonate call to anyone nearby. The RMC yearbook contained photos of each member of the graduating class with a brief description written by another member. It described me as having:

A slight English accent and a good sense of humor, although it sometimes runs to puns. His qualities as a leader soon brought him the hair graying honor of class senior. Essential to his Company 'E' in sports he was on both first hockey and rugby teams. Having a dead eye and considerable ability there is now a flourish of crossed rifles, guns, swords, and L.G badge when his left arm goes by.

I settled for this, knowing that less complimentary remarks might easily have been chosen instead.

The graduation exercises began on June 11 with the church parade to St. George's Cathedral in Kingston. This was followed by the graduation ceremonies the next day that were attended by all cadets, parents and family of the graduating class. My mother and father were there, and I felt very happy for them. I knew they were remembering the days they had spent at RMC when my father was on the College staff. Our diplomas were presented by the Minister of Labor, representing the Minister of National Defense. In his remarks he said, "there was never a time in the history of the world when it was more necessary for those who believe in the system of self-government and freedom to be ready for the acceptance of responsibility."

My friend Michael MacBrien won The Prince of Wales Cup for the best all-round athletics cadet during the course. I was awarded the Harris Bigelow Trophy – "for the member of the graduating class who displayed the best combination of academic and athletic ability throughout his entire course." I also obtained first prize in Mechanical Engineering and some nice comments from the Commandant in my report: "Very good work, is an all-around student and athlete with a pleasing personality, who should do well in the RAF." I felt pretty good about everything because I knew my parents were pleased. They had given me all the encouragement and support I needed. It was a day of celebration for them. My classmates and I were all proud of what we had done, but in each of our minds, there was some uncertainty, perhaps a small dark feeling about what we might face should there be a war. One doesn't know what lies ahead, but whatever it might be, I felt that RMC had prepared me well.

The great event that followed graduation was the RMC June Ball, and any worries we might have had about war were put aside for the time being. It was a brilliant weekend of dinner parties and picnics, and Bar came to be with me again. We arrived together at the ball at 10:30 P.M.. There were more than a thousand guests, including my parents and distinguished figures from across the country. They were received by the Commandant, Brigadier H.D.G. Crerar, Mrs. Crerar, and Battalion Sergeant Major Michael. D. MacBrien. The old Gymnasium was transformed into a ballroom with colorful decorations and streamers from the balcony, bayonets and lances on the walls, and sketches depicting life at the College. The dancing music was provided by the Bert Niosi Orchestra from Toronto, and my dance card was filled with Bar's name. The music was wonderful, and we danced to "Stardust," our favorite song. We loved the music, and the words seemed to tell how Bar and I felt being together again. "Sometimes I wonder why I spend the lonely nights dreaming of a song. The melody haunts my reverie, and I am once again with you."

The St. Lawrence Pier was decorated with large arches supporting red and white streamers. A waterfall and wheel beside the bathing shed gave the pier a festive feeling and a romantic setting for Bar and me. Supper was served at midnight in the mess hall, and the dancing concluded at 4 A.M. with the playing of "God Save the King." Bar and I went on to a breakfast party. Wow, what an evening it was!

*Ronald, Jimmy, Jean, Ronnie and Gertrude, in Tadoussac 1938.
(The last photo of the family together).*

SEVEN

LEARNING TO FLY

Immediately on leaving RMC, I began my pilot training. The situation in Europe was looking darker, and to many, the question was not "Will there be a war?" but "When?" While I was focused on learning to fly, I couldn't avoid reading the newspapers, filled daily with what was happening in Europe.

Germany had annexed Austria the year before, in the spring of 1938, and in September, Hitler had demanded that parts of Czechoslovakia become part of Germany. People in Britain and France were reluctant to go to war. They still lived with the horrible memory of the Great War and the loss of a generation of youth. Canadians felt the same, but we knew that if Britain went to war with Germany, Canadians would be in it, too. The Prime Minister, Mackenzie King, was reported in the Montreal Star as saying, "Canada is ready at any time to play her full part alongside democratic countries of the world."

After meeting Hitler in Munich last September, Britain's Prime Minister, Sir Neville Chamberlain, returned to London and announced an agreement and that "Peace in our time is assured." However, the situation continued to deteriorate, and an article in the *Montreal Gazette* explained how "Britain and France would give full armed assistance to Poland in case of aggression by Germany."

What was of particular interest to me were reports on how France and Britain were training their Air Force with mock bombing raids. In July, the *Montreal Star* had a story that because "Britain's heavy and medium bomber squadrons were now too fast for operations only in Britain, they were extending their flights to central and western France, to get experience in seeking targets. France was sending some of her bombing squadrons on mock raids over Britain."

During my pilot training, we talked about what a war might be like for pilots like us. My colleagues came from all over the country and had a wide range of views on Hitler and the likelihood of war. I discussed all this with my father because I felt he was realistic and much better informed than most. He told me war would now be difficult to avoid.

Canada's pilot training had been re-organized by the Royal Canadian Air Force, apparently to follow the RAF in England. For the initial stage, everyone was assigned to one of the numerous flying clubs in the country. I went to the Toronto Flying Club whose aerodrome was in North Toronto at Dufferin Street and Wilson Avenue. It was a good place to begin training because there was lots of activity. In early August I attended the Air Pageant in Goderich, Ontario, west of Toronto on the shore of Lake Huron. My training involved maneuvers and formations, a climbing and gliding competition, spot landings, parachute jumping and aerobatics.

The next stage was at the Service Flying Training School at the RCAF Station at Camp Borden. This was about 75 miles north of Toronto in Edenvale, west of Barrie. The relief landing fields located nearby consisted of either grass or asphalt runways, one hangar, and maintenance facilities.

Barracks for overnight stays allowed pilot trainees to conduct circuit training on landing and taking off in their airplane. Those in training came from Canada and from other parts of the Empire, including Australia, New Zealand, and Britain. Some were training to be pilots, others to be navigators, air gunners or flight engineers.

By the end of August, I had finished this first part of my training and was ready for the next stage at Trenton, Ontario, before earning my wings. I had been staying at my parents' home in Toronto for much of the time, which gave me the opportunity to see them; something I had not been able to do in all my years at school and college.

My father was very busy with his work, but I was able to have good conversations with him. He felt the world situation was likely to get worse and suggested that, before I took the next part of my training, this would be a good time for us to get away somewhere together. We drove north to Algonquin Park in Northern Ontario for a few days of canoeing and fishing. On that first evening, we pitched our tent beside a lake and settled in to enjoy the quiet of this peaceful place. The next morning, the ranger arrived at our camp with the news that war had been declared. It was September 3. My father had to return to Toronto immediately to mobilize the troops, many of whom had been trained in his district. Our fishing trip would have to wait.

I returned to my training with a new sense of urgency. War was now certain, and my career with the RAF took on a new sense of reality. Of course, we didn't know what might happen next. As District Commanding Officer, my father was immediately responsible for organizing troops under his command and preparing them to go overseas, while my mother helped with their families. In Toronto, the number of troops being mobilized increased from fifteen to fifty thousand.

We knew that Germany had invaded Poland on September 1. Two days later, these words came from the British Prime Minister, Neville Chamberlain:

> *I am speaking to you from the cabinet room at 10 Downing St. This morning, the British Ambassador in Berlin handed the German Government a final note stating that unless we*

heard from them by eleven o'clock that they were prepared at once to withdraw their troops from Poland, a state of war would exist between us. I have to tell you now that no such undertaking has been received and that consequently this country is at war with Germany.

I thought it was significant that although Britain had declared war, it did not declare war on behalf of Canada. The Canadian Parliament independently approved a declaration of war and asked King George VI to sign it. William Lyon Mackenzie King, the Prime Minister, announced Canada's Declaration of War, saying:

For months – indeed for years – the shadow of impending conflict in Europe has been ever present. Through these troubled years no stone has been left unturned, no road unexplored in the patient search for peace. Unhappily for the world, Herr Hitler and the Nazi regime in Germany have persisted in their attempt to extend their control over other peoples and countries, and to pursue their aggressive designs in wanton disregard of all treaty obligations, and peaceful methods of adjusting international disputes.
They have had to resort increasingly to agencies of deception, terrorism, and violence. It is this reliance upon force, this lust for conquest, this determination to dominate throughout the world which is the real cause of the war that today threatens the freedom of mankind.

My pilot training picked up the pace. Everything was on the move, and my next step was to obtain my "wings." This was at Trenton, Ontario, situated west of Kingston and north of Lake Ontario. The aircraft used in pilot training included the Harvard, the Fairey Battle and the Oxford. The Harvard was a single engine American airplane designed for training pilots for the Air Force, and Canada was now building them. They provided a transition from the low-powered and primary trainers such as the Tiger Moth, to the high-performance frontline fighters, such as the Hurricane and the Spitfire that would soon be used in the war. The Fairey Battle was a single engine British bomber introduced in the mid-thirties. The Oxford, a twin-engine aircraft, was introduced for training British Commonwealth aircrews in navigation, radio-operating, bombing and gunnery roles. I took my final Wings test in a Harvard aircraft and on November 23, we were presented with our "wings." There were 27 pilots in my class.

I had completed my pilot training after a total of 148 flying hours on the Harvard and the Battle, both single engine aircraft. I came second in the pilot class and was awarded the Sir John Siddeley Trophy for the pilot officer who obtained "the highest aggregate marks for both qualities as a pilot and practical work during the advanced training stage." I left Trenton and in January 1940, I returned to Camp Borden to take a course in navigation. This was the final part of my training with the RCAF before I crossed the Atlantic and reported to the RAF, where I received further training.

Our friends and their families were now focused on who might be leaving for England and when, and the roles they would play in the war. Many of my RMC classmates had been assigned to their units. On September 3, we were shocked by the news that the passenger liner, S.S. *Athenia*, had been torpedoed off Northern Ireland by a German submarine. She was on her way from Glasgow to Montreal. Most of the 1,347 passengers were Canadian or American and 117 of its passengers and crew were lost, including a ten-year old Canadian girl, Margaret Hayworth.

There was wide coverage in the news and at Camp Borden we talked about it and agreed it was a war crime to sink a passenger vessel with civilians. I thought about what could happen to ships carrying troops across the Atlantic.

During the months that followed Germany's invasion and bombing of Poland, very little had happened on the Continent. Canada was actively preparing for its part in war and the prospect of going overseas prompted action that was happy news. My sister Jean became engaged to John Aylan-Parker, a lieutenant in the Royal Canadian Regiment (RCR), soon to be promoted and called to go overseas. Their wedding was planned for November 18 at St. Simon's Church in Toronto, and I was to be one of their ushers. After graduating from Bishop's University, Johnny was interviewed by my father and recommended for the RCR. I would get to know him much better when we were both in England.

Bar planned to be at Jean's wedding until another surprise announcement came. My good friend, Ted Price, had become very taken with Bar's sister, Mary, and they too became engaged. Ted had joined the RCR and was called up to go overseas at the end of November with barely two weeks of notice. Their wedding was planned quickly for November 18 at St. George's Church in Montreal, the same day as Jean and Johnny's wedding in Toronto. Bar could not be at both. We were disappointed and so was Jean, but of course Bar was at her sister's wedding.

Jean's wedding was wonderful. She looked radiant and was full of her usual confidence. We had been so close as brother and sister growing up and I was very happy for her. She had recovered from her awful accident in Tadoussac at the end of the summer in 1938 when she had gone on a picnic with friends Peggy and Billy Tyndale and John Henderson to Moulin Baude. A few miles northeast of town the Baude River flows over a steep cliff, falling about sixty feet to the shore of the St. Lawrence River. As Jean crossed the top of Baude River, she slipped and fell down the falls. She grabbed onto a log in the pool at the bottom to avoid being carried out onto the big river. The others climbed down to rescue her and helped her back up the cliff. She was brought back to our house where a doctor gave her twenty stitches on her face, with no anesthetic. When I saw her, she looked like she'd been hit by a baseball bat, but she hadn't lost her wit and said: "I still think I am better looking than you." She had bitten through her lower lip, but the damage to her head was unknown. At the time, we didn't know how or if she might come through it all.

As I looked at her now on her wedding day, I found it hard to believe that this had ever happened. She looked wonderful and her lively spirit was shining for everyone to see. My grandfather was there to conduct the marriage. The reception afterwards was at my parents' home on Highland Avenue in Toronto. Johnny's fellow officers from the RCR gave a toast to the bride and Jean made a very nice speech. Ronnie was busy passing food around while I attached tin cans, old boots and other odds and ends to the back of their car to attract attention as they drove away on their honeymoon. Johnny sailed to England right after the wedding and Jean followed him soon after Christmas.

Bar's friends were also getting married before their husbands went overseas. Anne Winslow-Sprague married Donald Byers and Bar was a bridesmaid at their wedding. My cousins, Nan and Jackie Wallace were preparing to go overseas. Nan was a nursing sister in the Royal Canadian Medical Corps. Jackie would soon join the Artillery. My Uncle Sydney Williams was rector of the Church in Shawinigan Falls, Quebec. He wanted to go as a chaplain, but when this didn't happen, he went as a combatant officer in the Artillery.

Meanwhile, I was finishing my pilot navigation training. It put strict demands on my time, and I tried to find ways to be with Bar, who was in Montreal. I missed being with her, and I knew I would be going overseas very soon.

When she met our Samoyeds, Nick and Galka, she loved them. Her parents had two Airedales at their farm, and I told her she ought to have her own dog. She agreed immediately, so we found an Irish terrier puppy and we called him Okie, after my middle name, Okeden. He was the cutest and most gentle dog and Bar's parents took to him immediately. He lived with them in the city and traveled out to their farm in Sainte Thérèse, where they kept Stocky and Mac, the Airedales.

Christmas in 1939 felt unsettled. Our friends were making commitments and didn't know when they might be called up. However, a happy occasion was the RMC Christmas dance, and it was the custom to invite recent graduates to come back to the College. I went down to Kingston from Toronto and Bar came up from Montreal to join me. She had attended RMC dances with me for two years and felt right at home. We had a wonderful time. I had known for some time that I was deeply in love with Bar, and I wanted to spend my future with her. I knew, with my RAF career it might be a while before we could get married, but perhaps I should propose, and we could become engaged.

At Christmas, Bar went to Montreal to be with her family, and I was with my parents in Toronto. I enjoyed the time with Jean and my little brother. Ronnie was growing up quickly and he asked me lots of questions about airplanes and tanks. He would have his ninth birthday in August. Jean was preparing to leave for England and was excited about being there with Johnny. I didn't know when I would be going, but it would be as soon as possible after I finished my training. We all knew it would be our last Christmas together for a while.

In early January, a troublesome situation put my RAF career plans in question. I was finishing my navigation course in Trenton and my father wrote to me expressing his concern that we had not received information from the RAF about my status. I had been told that my commission would start on the date of my graduation in June 1939 and that I would follow the required training before being called over to England. Because I was the first RMC cadet to have ever been offered a commission directly out of the College, we thought that perhaps there was no earlier path for the paperwork to follow. My father wrote to G.M. Croll, Air Vice-Marshall, RCAF, in Ottawa who replied immediately saying that a request had been sent to the RAF for clarification, but that if the RAF did not wish to accept my services, I would be offered a permanent commission in the RCAF with seniority from the original date. That was some consolation, at least.

In a few weeks we received notice from the RAF that it was "not in a position" to accept me for Permanent Commission, but that I could be granted a commission in the RAF Volunteer Reserve for the duration of the War and then considered with others if vacancies existed in the peacetime establishment. It was clear that my father was not going to settle for this. He knew from the last war that many excellent officers were de-commissioned because of a reduced peacetime service and saw my commitment to the RAF as a full-life career, not just wartime service. I had been approved by the RAF before the war began and he considered this RAF action as a breach of faith with Royal Military College and with me the candidate. He wrote to Harry Crerar, who was the RMC Commandant when I graduated, and who was now at Army General Staff in England. They knew each other well so he didn't hesitate to ask him for some help. He also wrote to Air Vice-Marshall Croll in Ottawa, thanking him for his help and for the offer to me of a Permanent Commission in the RCAF. He wanted Croll to know that the choice of the RAF had been a serious one because he explained that, among the factors affecting the decision that I go into the RAF, was that I will one day inherit a nice-sized property in England, if there is anything left to inherit after this war. He also stressed that I had been accepted by the RAF for a Permanent Commission while at RMC and that this was a breach of faith on the part of the British Air Ministry with a Canadian candidate.

Depending on the response we received from the RAF, I would have to decide what to say to the Air Ministry in Ottawa about the RCAF offer. My father and I discussed it fully and agreed on a plan. My commanding officer at Trenton sent this telegram message to Ottawa:

> PILOT OFFICER ALEXANDER NOT INTERESTED IN RAF VOLUNTEER RESERVE COMMISSION; WOULD ACCEPT PERMANENT COMMISSION IN RCAF IF ABSOLUTELY DEFINITIVE THAT PERMANENT RAF COMMISSION NOT POSSIBLE; BUT FEELS THAT AS ORIGINAL APPOINTMENT WAS FOR RAF PERMANENT, THAT EVERY ENDEAVOR SHOULD BE MADE TO OBTAIN RECONSIDERATION OF HIS CASE WITH A VIEW TO OBTAINING SPECIAL CONSIDERATION FOR THE RAF PERMANENT.
> UNDERSIGNED C.A.S (IS CONVERSANT WITH THIS CASE).

The uncertainty continued into February. My father wrote to the new Commandant of RMC, Brigadier K. Stuart, and enlisted his help. Letters went back and forth to General Crerar in England, who replied that he had taken steps. On March 15, a telegram came from General Crerar saying:

> GLAD INFORM YOU AIR MINISTRY HAVE RECONSIDERED CASE JIM STOP AND AM ADVISED WILL ACCEPT NOMINATION PERMANENT COMMISSION RAF STOP OTTAWA NOTIFIED. –CRERAR

I was happy and relieved. Thank goodness my father had jumped in to help. He felt strongly about it; but knowing that he had once preferred that I go into the Army and the Artillery, his support meant so much to me. I have often wondered about another cadet in my position, who didn't have a father with the interest and the connections to make it happen.

After I received the good news, things moved quickly. I completed my navigation course in Trenton and received orders to go overseas and report to the RAF. I would take the train to Halifax and sail for England on March 28. This left me time to be with my parents and my brother in Toronto. Easter was on March 24 and Bar arrived on the evening train from Montreal to stay with us.

I wanted so much to be married to Bar, and I knew she felt the same about me. We had talked about it often and we felt it had to be now or possibly never. We would have been married right then, but the RAF did not permit Pilot Officers to get married unless they had permission from their Commanding Officer.

I had no idea who my Commanding Officer would be, and I wouldn't know until I reported for duty in England. I wanted to be prepared, so I went to Henry Birks & Sons jewelers in downtown Toronto and found a lovely engagement ring. It had three small diamonds set in platinum and inside, was the inscription: "Jimmy to Bar `40." We became officially engaged when Bar arrived to stay with us at Easter. It was all very exciting, and my parents were very happy. They liked Bar very much. When Bar and I told my mother we were engaged to be married, she said "good" and went upstairs. She soon returned, saying she'd taken off her girdle. Now that Bar was joining the family, she could be more comfortable.

I am not sure what Ronnie made of it all. He thought Bar was pretty good. She was fun for him, and I know she liked him. Our time together at my parents' home in Toronto was short but very happy. A late winter snowstorm filled the streets and sidewalks with snow, covering the spruce trees in white. It looked more like Christmas than Easter. Bar and I threw snowballs outside and walked my parents' black Scottie, Jock, as the snowflakes continued to fall lightly on us. It was a lovely neighborhood on a quiet street. Bar was full of life and laughter. I took photos of her with my movie camera. It was hard to imagine being happier. We both knew that we would be apart for some time, but the excitement of getting married helped us to think more about that.

In the evenings, we played bridge with my parents. Bar was so at ease with my mother and father, and we had lots of laughs. I had collected some playing records of songs by Paul Robeson. I loved his voice. We played "Stardust," the song Bar and I loved and danced to, written by Hoagy Carmicheal. The Easter weekend flew by, and we were so happy being together. Bar wanted to come over to England right away to be with me, but we agreed that she should wait until I got there, and I was able to get permission for us to be married.

On March 26, the day I left Toronto, Canada had a general election, and Prime Minister Mackenzie King and the Liberal Party were re-elected. He was an experienced Prime Minister and had the confidence of the country, although his election campaign included a promise not to impose conscription because of the need to keep the country united and the intense pressure in Quebec. I found an editorial in the Toronto newspaper that explained Canada's predicament:

> *We know that if the full force of the country's manpower is to be brought into play it must be based on a united national conviction. There is no doubt about the ardent feeling in a province like Ontario with racial roots in British traditions and where thousands of heirs of the United Empire Loyalist sentiment reside. A multitude of citizens can be found throughout the country with a similar attitude toward the*

Mother Country. On the other hand, we have the French Canadians, equally concerned for the freedom assured by British institutions but without the same background. We have also a large percentage of population which came to this country since the last war from non-British countries and lacking the urge to go back to Europe to fight for a cause sponsored by a nation to which allegiance has no direct appeal. These things have to be taken into account in seeking an undivided national effort. We are convinced that the Government, fortified by a unanimous Parliament, intends to prosecute the war with all its vigor, and that nothing essential to a successful conclusion will be neglected, not even conscription. It is to be remembered that the struggle has only started, and we have yet to get into it properly. The administrative machinery will need many amendments and changes, which will be forthcoming and changes in the situation abroad may mean changes here.

I was focused on what lay before me, starting with a long trip by train to Halifax. Nonetheless, when reading this I was encouraged, and I felt confident that Canada would live up to the reputation it had earned for courage and commitment during the last Great War.

PART TWO
Love and War

James O. Alexander, 1940.

Jimmy and Aunt Isabel, at Stutton House, Suffolk, England.

EIGHT

OFF TO WAR
April 1940

My mother never liked goodbyes. Every time I went back to boarding school, and then college, it was hard for her. She always wanted to get it over with quickly. Perhaps she didn't like the ceremony or formality, but I think it's more likely that she wanted to hide her emotions. I was sure that she felt quite deeply. She just didn't want to show it. That morning, when I left for England to begin my career with the RAF, I knew she loved me, but rather than seeing me off on the train, she kissed me goodbye before I left the house for the station.

I had mixed feelings as I left. I was excited to go overseas but emotional about leaving family and Bar. My father and Bar came to Union Station to see me off. There were many others in uniform saying goodbye. Before I boarded the train, Dad gave me a hug and a slap on the back. We didn't know when we would see each other again. Bar and I had plans, however and hoped she would be able to join me very soon. It was difficult for all of us at that moment, not knowing how long we would be away from each other.

The train took a day and a half to travel the 1200 miles to Halifax. The trip was interesting, especially beyond Montreal and Quebec City. Here, the track followed the south shore of the St. Lawrence River. A recent snowstorm made everything white and sparkling in the March sun. Across the deep blue of the river, I could see the mountains of the north shore that I knew so well in summer. I had brought my movie camera with me and took some good shots of the river, the snowy mountains and a dog pulling a sleigh across a field like our Samoyeds do.

When we arrived in Halifax, I was amazed at how busy it was. There were troops everywhere who had traveled from cities and towns across the country and were waiting for convoys to take them across the Atlantic to England. Convoys of fifty to sixty ships were escorted by corvettes and frigates of the Royal Canadian Navy to protect them from German submarines.

The Port of Halifax has a sheltered anchorage that can hold about one hundred and fifty ships. Looking out over the harbor, I began to appreciate the scale of what was involved in moving troops and arms across the Atlantic. My ship was delayed two days because she had made an unscheduled stop in St. John's, Newfoundland, on her crossing from England. She was the Canadian Pacific liner, *Duchess of York*, once a beautiful white, now a dirty grey for camouflage on the seas. I met two RCAF chaps reporting to their units in England and we boarded as a group. We went down to Pier 21 and got on a harbor tender which took us out and alongside the *Duchess*. Eight Army lads were with us on the tender and most of them seemed rather drunk, particularly the Major in charge. When we pulled alongside the *Duchess*, we climbed a rope ladder and nearly lost the Major. He managed to get aboard safely, but dropped some papers overboard, including one of his lad's passports.

The *Duchess* weighed anchor early on March 29. A convoy traveled at around ten knots to accommodate the slowest vessels and keep them together for protection. Because the *Duchess* could make a speed of about twenty knots, we proceeded alone across the Atlantic.

A thick fog shrouded the first three days at sea, and we had little visibility. The ship's horn made a low resonating sound that must have carried a long distance. It sounded all the time, and I kept hoping that a German sub would not hear it. I had a first-class cabin because I was an officer. Among the other passengers on the ship, I came upon Phyllis Henshaw whom I had known in Quebec and who was traveling with another girl. She was going over to marry Harry Boswell. We all played bridge, ping pong and bet on the horse races. Lady Tweedsmuir, the widow of Lord Tweedsmuir, was also on the ship. He had died in February after being Governor General of Canada for five years. I felt sad for Lady Tweedsmuir as her husband had been a remarkable man. I would not forget his lecture at RMC on T. E. Lawrence.

There were also some Royal Navy lads on board, and we played bingo one evening. It was important for me to keep moving, so I played deck tennis outside and walked around the decks for a bit of exercise. There was also a gym on board. Most of what we needed was covered by our passage ticket, but we could also make purchases in British sterling on board. I had never used sterling before, and I was able to change Canadian dollars at the purser's office.

After a few days the ship emerged from the fog into bright sunshine, but the sea was rough, and some people took to their cabins. The way the ship rolled I understood why she was called a "drunken Duchess." Watching the water slosh around in my bathtub confirmed how rough it was. I didn't realize it was saltwater until I got it in my eyes.

The weather improved, and the sun was quite warm, even though our course took us far north on the Atlantic.

The ship was now zigzagging on her course and, as we came closer to England, we were told that we had entered the high danger area, out of range of defensive aircraft protection. Here was where we were most likely to encounter German U-boats. We were asked to always carry our life belts, and on the final day we were given gas masks to take ashore when we arrived at Liverpool.

During the entire six-day crossing we hadn't seen another ship, and pulling into the Mersey, I wondered how that was possible. I had never seen so many ships and docks. Liverpool was a hive of activity and its landmark, the Liver building with its massive clock stood over it all. I was excited and thought of how I had left here, as a baby, twenty-one years ago at the end of another war.

It was April 4, and I thought of Bar, knowing that by now she would be back home in Montreal with her parents. I wrote to her every day of the voyage, but of course I couldn't post my letters until we landed in England. At least she would have some idea what to expect when she made her own voyage. I said I hoped it would be very soon.

When we came ashore, there seemed to be little if any organization for our arrival and we boarded a train for London. I was in a first-class compartment with three other passengers, but my friends were in third class, so I joined them. Everything seemed so green compared to what I had left at home. Spring had arrived and as the train traveled through the countryside I was struck by how small, neat and tidy everything looked. The rows of new houses were all the same and I thought them rather hideous.

When we arrived in London, I was struck by the thousands of chimney pots. We were met by two girls in Air Force uniforms and a young lad who handled our luggage, which he piled on a truck that drove away. Another girl from the Air Force drove us to our hotel, The Cumberland, near Marble Arch. When she asked what I wanted to see most in London, I said, "a black-out," and she laughed.

Now that I was in London, I settled comfortably in a rather nice hotel, a bit more expensive than I needed, but I didn't expect to be there for long. I was sure that the RAF would have immediate plans for me.

That evening, I found out what a blackout was like. It was April and the days were getting longer, so it didn't get dark until about 8:30 P.M. Suddenly all the streetlights were switched off. Traffic lights were covered as were automobile headlights and heavy curtains blocked all light from windows. There were candles in the Underground stations. It was eerie and walking along a street you might bump into another person. Stepping off the sidewalk could be especially dangerous, although white stripes were often painted on the curbs. London had not been bombed yet, but it was prepared.

The next morning, along with my two Air Force pals, I went to the RCAF Headquarters. It was located on Cockspur Street near Trafalgar square and next to Canada House, a building designed by Sir Robert Smirke, the same architect who built the British Museum. I had never seen such beautiful Greek Revival architecture. The other two were immediately assigned to a training facility and would be leaving the next day. I walked from Trafalgar Square along the Strand to Aldwich and Kingsway to the British Air Ministry in Adastral House and reported in. I was told that I should go to see the RAF medical officer. They had not yet received all my papers, and they suggested I do whatever I needed to do in London during the next few days while waiting. They were very nice and quite concerned that I might feel I wasn't being welcomed.

While at RCAF headquarters earlier that morning, I had met Group Capt. Welsh, who knew my father. He invited me to have lunch with him and took me to the United Service Club on Pall Mall, known by its members as the "Senior" because it was used by senior officers of the Royal Navy and Army. Afterwards we walked over to the Royal Over-Seas League for a coffee. It is located on Park Place, off St. James's Street. I discovered that two of my RMC classmates, Hugh Morrisey and "Pip" Nation were staying there.

I took a long walk that afternoon. It was a mostly sunny day, and I felt so pleased to be in London. While growing up, I had thought of it as the great city and capital of the British Empire. I wasn't disappointed. Although I left England when I was six months old, I felt British. When I spoke to people I had met at the Air Ministry, I wondered what they thought of my accent and if I might have a little of my father's English accent. My classmates at RMC mentioned it sometimes. I am sure that I sounded different to the English and most likely they would identify me as a Canadian.

My father had given me several pages of names and addresses of people I might want to meet in England. Some were my Parry-Okeden cousins, others were friends, including his former Army colleagues. He even suggested the best shops to get things I might need. I walked up to Piccadilly Circus, along Piccadilly Street, passing by Fortnum & Mason where people were going in to have their afternoon tea, and to Green Park. I took a bus up Park Lane to Marble Arch where I walked over to where I was staying at the Cumberland Hotel. That evening, I made some telephone calls. I tried to ring my sister and discovered that she didn't have a phone. I sent her a wire saying I had arrived and asked her to be in touch. I rang Aunt Isabel in Suffolk. She was so excited to hear from me so soon after I had arrived and said that my voice sounded just like my father's. She told me that her daughter Gwen (St. John) was in London. I rang her and we arranged to meet in a day or two. Aunt Isabel was married to my grandmother's brother, Uncle Herbert Parry-Okeden. He had served in the Great War and died in 1930. Aunt Isabel continued to live at Stutton House, their family home in Suffolk. My father had spent time there while on leave during the Great War. Gwen and my father were first cousins and were very close, like brother and sister. I knew that someday, I might inherit the Stutton estate. This fact never seemed important to me, even though I saw how beautiful it was. But soon I would enjoy times there with Bar, Aunt Isabel, and sometimes Gwen.

My first few days in London were busy with settling matters. I wrote a long letter to Bar. I told her how much I missed her and everything I was doing; but in particular I told her how much I wanted her to come over. On Monday morning I went back to the Air Ministry and took my medical. I came out with top marks so there were no worries there. After this I was interviewed by various training people and told I would be going on a course somewhere in England, but they couldn't tell me where it would be. I expected I would be flying the Fairey Battle aircraft again, which didn't thrill me because I had been flying them already and I wanted to fly something new. They asked me if I wanted to fly fighters, but I said I'd prefer to fly bombers. I had read articles in the newspapers recently saying that it would be important for an RAF fighter force to be able to defend against German bombing. However, I told them that I would prefer to be in long range bombing. I wondered if I might be sorry for this choice, but I knew that whatever happens anything can turn out well if you make a sincere effort of it. I wasn't certain, of course, but I felt that bombers might be the most important force in modern warfare. Thinking of my career in the RAF, I was more comfortable with my choice of long-range bombers over fighters.

My Training wouldn't start for a while, so I had a couple of weeks to get in touch with people. I called my brother-in-law, Johnny Aylan-Parker, and went down to see him and Jean. They had a nice little house in the village of Aldershot, which they shared with another couple, the Stevens. I stayed overnight and Johnny took me to the RCR mess for lunch. Jean and I went for a long bicycle ride in the afternoon. It was awfully nice to see her, and I hoped she wouldn't mind if I went down to see her again. I also saw HEC (Ted Price). He and Bar's sister Mary were living in Wickham, a village further southwest towards Portsmouth. I was with them on the morning of April 9 when we heard the news on the radio that the Germans had occupied Denmark and invaded Norway. Many were shocked at Germany's invasion of a neutral country. There had been no fighting since the Germans had invaded Poland and war had been declared last September. Now there was talk that the

Canadians might be sent to defend Norway. If Ted had to go with RCR, Mary said it would be wonderful if Bar came over to keep her company. I thought it would be better for Bar to wait until I knew when we could get married. Bar had a very good friend in Norway. She and Elisabeth Hoegh had been at school together in Marlow, near London. What would happen to Elisabeth now, we might never know.

I traveled back on the train to London that night and arrived in the blackout. When I arrived at Waterloo station, I got lost and landed in some back street. With some help I found a taxi back to the Cumberland Hotel. I laughed and thought how much fun it would have been getting lost and having Bar with me. The blackout had been imposed in September 1939, when war was declared, and they had expected Germany to bomb the cities. They were a fearful reminder that we were at war and that something terrible might happen any minute. And yet it wasn't happening. Since September 1939, there had been no bombing on England or by the RAF on Germany, except for dropped leaflets. The Prime Minister, Neville Chamberlain, called it the "Phony War" and the British carried on. The news this morning of Germany's invasion of Norway would probably change things. People wondered what would happen next. I felt sure the Germans would be stopped before they got very far.

When I arrived back at my hotel, there was a message from my cousin Gwen. She had been by earlier in the day and had invited me to go to the theatre with her and Mr. and Mrs. Buchan. Mr. Buchan was the son of Lord Tweedsmuir. I was sorry to miss this. The next day I ran into General Crerar on the street in London. He said he was never too busy to see me, and I thanked him again for helping to clear up the mess with my RAF commission. That afternoon, Gwen and Mrs. Wallace, a good friend who referred to my father as the "Briggydeer," took me to a play at the Aldwych Theatre. It was the comedy "Nap Hand." I thought it extremely funny and rather broad, even for London. It will certainly never appear anywhere in Canada. My father had told me that the Wallaces had been in touch with him to see whether he and my mother could look after their ten-year-old son, Simon, if he came out to Canada for the duration of the war. Many parents in England wanted to find safety for their young children with families in Canada. My parents were not able to take this on because their movements were uncertain, however my Uncle Jack and Aunt Mary Wallace agreed to look after Simon who was the same age as their son, Michael. Coincidentally, they had the same last name but were not related to each other.

Letters from home were very important to me, especially those from Bar. I wanted to be sure that everything was in place so I would receive them. All mail was being sent to me c/o the Bank of Montreal at Waterloo Place. The RAF would likely have me moving around to different places which were not on the regular postal routes of the Royal Mail, and some might be protected for security. The Bank of Montreal would be my point of communication with home. It offered this service to its Canadian clients when they were in England.

There was little traffic on the streets as I walked to the bank. Once there, I introduce myself to a Miss Crow. She gave me a friendly welcome and when I mentioned my father's name to her, she practically told me my whole family history. I told her that I was hoping to receive letters from home, and that I wrote to my parents often and to my fiancé almost every day. She seemed to understand. She handed me a letter that had just arrived. It was from Elspeth Laird, a great friend of my mother, who she had grown up with in Quebec City. Enclosed was a check for £10 to spend as I liked. I went immediately to Austen-Reed's on Regent Street and ordered my Air Force tunic and slacks. I also bought a pair of golf shoes from a Lotus shop. I was getting to know a part of London quite well, but I had yet to try the Underground.

The bus was very easy to use, and I could see where I was going. I had lunch at Lyons Cornerhouse on the Strand. There was lots of choice, no sign of rationing and the meals were reasonably priced and tasted good. I enjoyed exploring London, but I missed Bar so much and wanted her here so we could do things together. I wasn't working yet and was still waiting to hear about my training course. I didn't know anything about it or where it would be. I decided to keep busy by getting in touch with family and friends in England. I wrote to my Uncle Tim, my father's younger brother, and Aunt Coral. He was in the Essex Regiment. They invited me to go down to where they lived to do some pigeon shooting sometime, but I felt that I first wanted to make a visit to Stutton. I called Aunt Isabel and told her I would take the train to Ipswich and would come to see her. I recalled how often my father had talked about her and how much he loved Stutton, so I was quite excited about meeting her and seeing it. When I arrived, she greeted me as if I was her grandson and made me feel at home. I didn't stay long, but I fell in love with Stutton immediately and she suggested that I leave my trunk and other belongings there and return whenever I liked.

It was now a couple of weeks since I had first reported to the RAF, and I was beginning to feel a little frustrated that I had not heard anything. However, when things happen, they can happen quickly. I received a message from the Air Ministry to report immediately. I was soon immersed with RAF 98 Squadron, at a large base at Benson, forty-five miles west of London and twelve miles from Oxford. The base opened in 1939 and was designed for operational training for pilots, observers and air gunners on the Fairey Battles, the light bombing aircraft that were now being used by the RAF on the Continent. Several squadrons had completed their training already and had flown over to France as part of the Advanced Air Striking Force (AASF). When I arrived at Benson, I think the first question on my mind was to find out if my commanding officer would allow me to get married. As with the Army, junior officers in the RAF had to obtain permission from their commanding officer before getting married. When I asked him, he replied that he liked his officers to be married. I was thrilled and cabled Bar immediately. I think she tried to get on the next ship to England.

It turned out that Bar's departure from home was not so easy. Her parents were not against us being married, but they strongly objected to her coming over to England. Perhaps they felt that having both of their daughters in England during the war was too much to risk. During her childhood she had sometimes been at odds with her father, and I think she felt closer to her mother. We wanted so much to be together, and Bar was determined to come over to England; but her parents refused to pay her passage across, and Bar could not afford it on her own. This must have been difficult. Her friends gave her support and her old friend, Anne Byers, helped her pack her things.

Eventually, Bar was on her way. My career with the RAF had taken off, and we would soon be together again.

I found out later that my parents had paid for her passage.

Jimmy and Bar's wedding day, May 4, 1940.

NINE

LONDON
May 1940

It was the first of May 1940 when Bar arrived in England. Her ship docked at Liverpool, and she took the train to London. When I met her at Euston Station, she was radiant. We were so happy to be together again. It had been a month since I had left her in Toronto at Easter, but it seemed much longer. When I looked into her eyes, I could tell she had something important to tell me.

"We are going to have a baby!" she said.

At first, I was stunned, but then I was enormously happy. She explained that a few days before she left Canada, she had thought she might be pregnant, but she didn't say anything to anyone, especially to her parents. During her crossing she had become certain. We were full of joy but also worried about what our family back home would think if they knew. We decided not to tell them because it would be considered scandalous among many of the older generation. We had planned to be married as soon as possible after Bar arrived. With the war, weddings were happening at a moment's notice because no one knew when one might be called away. We needed to arrange for a church and a minister. While we didn't tell our parents or anyone else about the baby, we knew our sisters who lived nearby, would probably guess. Besides, we could use their help. So, we decided that Bar would tell Mary, and I would tell Jean. I had to stay on the base at Benson, while Bar was staying with Ted and Mary about an hour away. When I told my sister she said she would keep it a secret and wouldn't tell Johnny. We were able to arrange for our wedding to be held on Saturday at a church, three days after Bar arrived. I think that Mary had begun to think about planning our wedding as soon she heard that Bar was on her way across the Ocean. While everyone expected we would be married, they may have been surprised it was so soon.

Mary and Ted and Jean and Johnny were wonderful and made all the arrangements, but they knew Bar would have her own ideas. I had to apply to my Commanding Officer for forty-eight hours leave. The reason I gave was that my "best man," my brother-in-law Johnny, was due to be called over to the Continent with his regiment. On May 4, we were married in St. Mark's Church, South Farnborough, just north of Aldershot. Ted gave Bar away. The Clergyman was Captain Addie who was from Sherbrooke, Quebec, and a friend of my Uncle Sydney Williams. I had a simple gold wedding ring engraved on the inside with "Bar and Jimmy, May 1940." In the vestry afterwards, Bar and I signed the book along with Jean and Johnny and Mary and Ted. It was a small wedding, a simple service in a nice church, and we were fortunate to have a few friends there with us as well as Bar's cousins: Margaret and Evelyn Boosey and their children. Margaret had kindly offered to have it all at her home in Sevenoaks, Kent. However Ted had arranged for a reception at the Officer's Club in Aldershot, just down the road from St. Mark's Church. Mary got the cake. It was a beautiful day, and we were able to get some nice photographs taken outside the Church. Bar was wearing a blue and white dress, and I wore my RAF uniform. After the reception we left in a taxi for a very short honeymoon. I had to be back on the Base the next day.

Newly married, we settled into our little flat. It was not far from the base at Benson. There were very strict rules that wives and family must live away from the air Base. This is for safety reasons as the base would be a likely target of enemy bombing. It is something we would have to get used to wherever I was to be stationed. I was required to live on the base because often we had to be in a state of readiness, except when on leave. I was able to go home for meals at our flat, but neither Bar nor I had much experience cooking. We tried a rack of lamb, but we didn't know how long to cook it on our paraffin stove, so we took the mean between Bar's guess of time and mine. It all tasted very good, but we didn't have a carver, so we had to cut it with a bread knife. Our flat was likely to be our home for the next month until I would move out somewhere with my squadron, probably to France. We were both so pleased we had our sisters and their husbands near us, but we didn't know for how long. They were close family and good friends.

We received many lovely wedding gifts; some were kept in Canada for us until after the war. Bar's parents gave us our set of flat silver: a dozen knives, forks, spoons, etc., from Henry Birks & Sons, with the Alexander crest on them. Mrs. Hampson gave us linen. There were carpets, kitchenware, and other useful things, including some money from members of the family. Jean and Johnny gave us a radio. My parents asked what we would like as a wedding gift so I wrote and said we would find something here that we needed and let them know, but to tell Ronnie that we would love to have a "toast rack." Aunt Minnie gave us a silver ink stand, and I wrote to thank her. Bless her heart. She said she couldn't afford a check that would look big enough, but she thought the ink stand was quite valuable and if we didn't like it, we could sell it. It was a lovely gift.

We were so happy to be together again. Bar was feeling her pregnancy but managing well. We had already been talking about names. We hadn't settled on a girl's name, but if it was a boy I wanted to name him after my great friend at RMC, Michael MacBrien. Bar may have had other ideas, but she liked the name, and she remembered MacBrien from the times she had met him when she came to RMC. We decided on "Michael."

During this time, we were able to get a couple of days to go up to London. There had been a few sporadic bombing raids on England; none in London, but people were being prepared for what might come soon. The situation seemed more serious on the Continent. The newspapers reported that our troops had evacuated from Norway and the Norwegian King and government had been re-established in England. On May 10, we heard on the BBC news that the Prime Minister, Neville Chamberlain, had resigned and Winston Churchill had been asked by the King to form a new government. The *London Daily Telegraph* reported that Churchill, in addition to being Prime Minister, would also act as Minister of Defense, supervising the three Service Ministries, the Royal Navy, the Army and the RAF. He was a controversial figure and not everyone was comfortable having him as Britain's leader in what was going to be a very challenging time. Also, on the same day, Germany invaded Belgium, France, Luxembourg and Holland and according to the Sunday *Observer:*

> *The enemy struck into both the Low Countries at three o'clock in the small hours of Friday morning with the intent to murder two more nations in their sleep.*
>
> *As in Poland, Denmark, and Norway the Nazi air-technique led the onslaught. Their bombers ranged far and wide over the immediately assailed nations and into France to harass the Allied advance. They attacked civilian populations where it suited them.*

And the next day, the London Newspapers reported that British forces had occupied Iceland to secure it from a German invasion. At the time I didn't understand the significance of this, but within a few months I would.

Despite all this news, we were happy to be able to get up to London together, feeling fortunate to be able to enjoy it before anything further happened in the war. We did lots of walking; the weather was warm and lovely, and we strolled through Hyde Park and Green Park. People were enjoying themselves with picnics, children and dogs were playing, others were boating, and some were swimming in the Serpentine. The parks were not busy. We walked past Buckingham Palace and stopped to watch the King's Guards, dressed in their red tunics and busby headdress, which is made of black bearskin from Canada. Nearby, in St. James's Park, we sat on the grass and watched the ducks, geese, and swans swimming in the large ponds. The shrubs were still flowering, and the gardens were in bloom. I thought of my mother and how much she would have appreciated it all. Green Park is beautiful, and it felt so peaceful in a time of war. We passed by 10 Downing Street and walked over to Westminster Abbey and the Parliament buildings. There was Big Ben, so familiar from the photographs we had seen; and when it struck, the sound of it reminded us of Christmas, when the King spoke on the radio to all the British Empire. We found our way along the Embankment, where a variety of boats and crafts moved up and down the Thames. Turning up beside Charing Cross Station, we walked over to St. Martin-in-the-Fields and then along the Strand by the Savoy Hotel and Simpson's Restaurant, famous for its roast beef and Yorkshire pudding, but we couldn't afford to eat there. In the evening there were many people out walking along the Strand. We stopped to watch an older man playing a piano accordion as people walked by. His accordion had a beautiful tone, even if it looked a bit old. We listened until he stopped playing and we asked him how he had learned to play. He was happy to talk with us and we were surprised when he offered to sell us the accordion for what seemed a very low price. We didn't know anything about accordions, but he told us it was a Hohner,

Carmen II, made in Germany, probably about fifty years ago. We bought it from him, and as we carried it away in its large black case, we laughed. Neither of us had any idea how to play it, but we would have something to work on together and Bar was soon playing "Polly Wally Doodle," one of her favorites.

Some mornings, Bar felt unwell because of her pregnancy, but she was always up and ready to go. The fun we had took our minds off the growing worries of war. People were going about as if everything was normal, despite the daily reports of German advances and air attacks on Luxembourg, Belgium and Holland. We both loved London, but we wondered if this might be the last time we would be able to enjoy it together. We didn't know where my squadron would be posted.

When we returned to Benson, I had to stay on the base during the next week for some very active training and a lot of flying. I knew I might be moving with my squadron soon, and probably to France. Until now, during the so called "Phony War," the RAF had been dropping pamphlets to affect civilian morale; but since the German attacks on the Low countries that had changed, and RAF bomber squadrons from the AASF in France were carrying out daily raids attacking the enemy and supporting our military on the ground. While the general view was that AASF squadrons were making their mark in action, lessons were being learned, and our training had the benefit of their experience. The Fairey Battle, the aircraft I was flying, had been introduced in 1937 and intended as a long-range strategic bomber, capable of flying over to the industrial Ruhr Valley and returning home. A single engine aircraft, its crew included a pilot, navigator and gunner. It carried a 250 lb. bomb at a speed of 257 mph, but was considerably slower than the German Me109 fighter which flies at 350 mph. Its 303 in. machine gun provided limited defense and while its light armor gave it more speed, there was less protection for its crew, and few of the Battles had been refitted with self-sealing fuel tanks to protect them from fires. During our training we became aware of all the features of our aircraft, both strengths and weaknesses. We were also aware that attempts to fly the Battles on low level attacks were resulting in some losses.

Another part of our training at Benson included the history of the RAF and the thinking behind bombing as an offensive strategy in modern war. Fighters would be important to defend against enemy bombing attacks; and to protect our bombers when on raids. Our training covered what was being learned from our recent attacks on enemy airbases, ports, shipping, troop movements, communications, and industry supporting their war effort. It also included what was known about the enemy's anti-aircraft capabilities and the Luftwaffe's Me 109 fighters. Flying in bad weather and at night was considered an important part of our flying ability. Reaching and returning from enemy targets requires that pilots know how to fly in all kinds of weather. Reliable predictions help, but when you are in the air for five to ten hours, the weather can change. There were frequent forced landings by pilots losing their way. Our daylight bombing raids had been taking large losses and night flying was becoming more essential. Pilots had to learn to fly in darkness and in bad weather. Our training was having a greater focus on navigation, aiming and dropping bombs, taking D/F (radio direction finding) bearings, and working a rotating D/F foil and a gun.

When they completed training at Benson, RAF officers were assigned to one of the three Operational Commands of the Air Force. As the strategic offense, Bomber Command was considered the core of the RAF; Fighter Command would support the Army land forces; Coastal Command would conduct shore defense and sea operations. Overall, the RAF now saw itself as the offensive instrument of the combined forces of the Army and Navy. I had chosen bombers over fighters for this reason. It was frequently argued that "the bombers would always get through."

As my training continued at Benson, I was doing more flying, and I think my CO was fairly satisfied with how I was doing. My flight commander was an Australian, a very nice person and I was in Squadron No.1, "A" Flight. We had the sense that things on the Continent were changing quickly. I hadn't done anything much so far, but I was pretty sure that some of us would be going over to the Continent and would see action very soon. Then on May 25 there were reports that German forces were driving the British Expeditionary Force (BEF) and French troops to the Coast. On May 31, The Daily Telegraph reported that thousands of BEF troops had been evacuated from Dunkirk on the coast of France by the Royal Navy and many small boats had brought them back to England. The newspapers reported that the RAF were successfully destroying German forces and communications on the ground, while at the same time, protecting our troops as they were being evacuated from the beaches. Many German aircraft were shot down. As the full story of events became clearer, there was grave concern that the BEF, a major part of Britain's army would be lost, and that only twenty to forty thousand might be saved. What happened turned out to be something quite different. Prime Minister Churchill told the House of Commons that 335,000 British and French troops had been successfully evacuated and transported across the Channel. He described it as "a miracle of deliverance" but said that the attribute of victory must not be assigned to it. On the contrary, he called it a "colossal military disaster." He reported the severe loss of the Army's military equipment, but he also noted that there was a victory inside it all that was gained by the RAF in its battle with the Luftwaffe. While people seemed jubilant; Churchill emphasized reality by saying, "Wars are not won by evacuations."

Dunkirk brought home to us the reality of war. If we were not already aware that Britain would be standing alone against a Germany that might soon occupy the entire continent of Europe,

Churchill made it clear to all when he spoke to Parliament:

> *We shall go on to the end, we shall fight in France, we shall fight on the seas and oceans, we shall fight with growing confidence and growing strength in the air, we shall defend our Island, whatever the cost may be, we shall fight on the beaches, we shall fight on the landing grounds, we shall fight in the fields and in the streets, we shall fight in the hills; we shall never surrender, and even if, which I do not for a moment believe, this Island or a large part of it were subjugated and starving, then our Empire beyond the seas, armed and guarded by the British Fleet, would carry on the struggle, until, in God's good time, the New World, with all its power and might, steps forth to the rescue and the liberation of the old.*

In the days that followed Dunkirk, and while I was still at Benson, Bar and I rode our bicycles around the neighborhood villages. We noticed that many army vehicles were driving through them, carrying weapons of one sort or another. This seemed a little strange as we thought it unlikely that enemy action was expected in this part of the country. We believed it was to assure the public that Britain still had sufficient military equipment to fight an invasion if it were to happen.

RMS Lancastria

*Sinking of RMS Lancastria, June 17, 1940.
St. Nazaire, France.*

TEN

FRANCE
June 1940

On June 1, Bar and I celebrated my twenty-second birthday. A gift from my 98 Squadron at Benson was news that I would be going to France at once. On June 4, I flew over to join RAF Bomber 98 Squadron at their base near Nantes.

After the evacuation of British and allied troops from Dunkirk, there was still an estimated 150 thousand British Army and RAF airmen who remained in France. The French Government had asked Churchill for help and for more RAF squadrons. Churchill had agreed saying that. *"The British Empire and the French Republic, linked together in their cause and in their need, will defend to the death their native soil, aiding each other like good comrades to the utmost of their strength."*

However, the Germans Panzer divisions and the Luftwaffe were continuing their push southward, and British and French forces were in retreat – and I was on my way to the war in France.

When I arrived at Nantes, the AASF had withdrawn to a base just outside the city of Orleans. There were six RAF bomber squadrons and three Hurricane fighter squadrons staying in France to attack the advancing German army and their lines of communications. 98 Squadron was now based at Chateau Bougon, about two hundred miles southwest of Orléans and just outside the city of Nantes on the Loire River. As soon as I arrived, the squadron was ordered to return to England, and by June 15 all our Fairey Battle and Blenheim aircrafts had gone, leaving the rest of us behind. We were fourteen flying officers and a ground crew of two hundred and thirty airmen. We were told to make our way to the coast where troop ships were waiting near the port of St. Nazaire at the mouth of the Loire River. We drove from Nantes to St. Nazaire which is only about thirty-five miles, and the roads were filled with people walking or driving toward the ports. There were French and Polish soldiers and many of ours from the British Expeditionary Force who had not been able to reach Dunkirk. Refugees, including women and children, babies, and pets from the north of France and Belgium were on the roads, hoping to be evacuated. Among them were undesirables ready to steal anything that wasn't guarded. Railways and communications were out of action, and it was a hot day on the roads. The Luftwaffe were bombing and firing on vehicles and on people as they walked, and they were bombing St. Nazaire when we arrived there. We gathered on the shore and, being the only one who could speak French, I got hold of a refugee, and he drove our kit down to one of the docks with his truck. We stood there watching the RAF lorries drive onto the beach right to the water's edge. To destroy them, the drivers put their engines in low gear and forward into the sea, jumping out at the last minute.

Large "troopships" were anchored well offshore, while destroyers, lighters and tenders ferried back and forth to them. We waited on shore while the bombing continued, but we were not directly affected. It was a lovely fireworks display that night, and early in the morning on June 17 we were taken out by tenders to board one of the two large troopships. They were painted a dull grey and had once been large passenger liners. We didn't know at first which ones they were, but once we were aboard, I overheard someone near me pointing to the ship's single funnel noting the grey painted over the familiar red and black stripes of a Cunard Liner. She was the RMS *Lancastria*, a 16,000-ton liner. She would normally have a capacity of 2,500 people including its crew. When we arrived, there were well over that number on board, and destroyers continued to bring more, possibly another 5,000 to 7,000. No-one knows for sure how many. We wondered why she was waiting so long before weighing anchor. Meanwhile, I was able to have a bath and a shave, and I felt much better.

About noon, we went down to lunch and during lunch we had about four separate raids. They hit the liner nearby, but didn't do much damage. Later, I heard that the ship was the SS Oronsay. After lunch, I went up to my cabin to have a sleep, but the two bunks were full. I cursed, little knowing how lucky I was, and went out onto the sun deck. What happened next was unexpected to say the least. Suddenly, out of the clouds came a couple of Jerry bombers. We opened fire with two Bren guns, but of course the bombers were too high, and we all got off the sundeck and onto the promenade. We hoped that RAF Hurricanes might be around to give us some protection, but we had seen them on shore, trying to protect retreating allies from the Luftwaffe and the advancing German army. A few Hurricanes flew over us as they returned home to refuel, and one of them shot down a German Ju 88. It did a slight victory roll displaying its RAF roundel and a red maple leaf on its side and flew off with cheers from our ship.

Suddenly, a big four-engine job came out of the clouds and dived on us. It dropped two bombs which hit the water about fifty yards away from the ship and went up in the clouds again. It soon returned and diving across us it dropped two more. They both hit us near the bridge. I ducked down as wood and splinters flew everywhere. The lad beside me on the deck was killed. One didn't have time to worry about him. When I stood up, I realized the ship was starting to list. What a feeling! I hurried back onto the open deck and a few of us officers tried to organize everyone. It was difficult, but we managed to keep the ship fairly even by all going from one side to the other until the ship listed to port at a forty-five-degree angle and began to sink. We were able to get only a few of the lifeboats down and some of them turned over and their occupants were thrown into the water. It was obvious that we would have to swim for it. People climbed over the rails, lowered themselves into the water and were immersed in a black slick of oil pouring from the side of the ship.

I took my wallet out of my tunic and put it in my trousers, and then I took my trousers off and threw them away. I climbed out on a davit and went down a rope with my underwear shorts, my socks, my watch and no life belt. In the water, I kicked off my socks and swam to a lifeboat and hung onto the side of it for about half an hour till I nearly froze. Someone in the lifeboat chucked me his lifebelt and I swam away. Many in the water were without life belts and could not swim. They were holding onto whatever they found floating as they cried for help. Survivors were spread out over a large area floating with the current. Heinkel bombers machine gunned those in the water and on lifeboats and dropped incendiaries to set fire to the oil on the water. I was Eventually rescued by a lifeboat belonging to a French trawler. When the trawler made toward us, she rammed us, and I was in the water again. However, I got back on the trawler and was more or less safe. I watched the old ship go down gracefully, and as she sank there were many clinging to her, including some lads sitting on the funnel singing "Roll Out the Barrel." I went into the water once again to rescue an old woman who was a refugee, and I got coated in oil.

Eventually, the trawler brought us to a destroyer. Many of those rescued were in terrible shape, covered in oil and suffering from burns or other wounds. Finally, our destroyer pulled away from Saint Nazaire, out of the Bay of Biscay and far around the Head of Brittany to avoid U-boats before reaching the English Channel. It took a while to get back to England, and eventually we arrived at Plymouth, in Devon on the southwest coast. We were wearing all kinds of clothing. Someone had given me a pair of trousers and a shirt. I had lost my wallet, my silver pencil, the flask which Bar had given me, and the Bible my grandmother gave me when I was young. I was still wearing my watch, and it worked. My camera was gone – a serious loss, because I had taken some pretty good movies in France. I went over to Austin Reed in Plymouth to get some new clothes, and I was able to talk to Bar on the phone. I caught the train up to London and she met me at Paddington station. I told her the whole story. I did not know how many lives were lost on the *Lancastria*. Possibly half of those on board were killed or drowned. When the bombs hit, many of the troops were resting in their cabins or eating in the dining hall and were unable to get up on deck to escape. I learned that my squadron lost ninety airmen and there were other RAF squadrons on the ship. I was relieved to hear that my friend Dick Shuttleworth had survived. We had joined 98 Squadron together in April.

I was able to get a room in London at Overseas House near St. James's Place for Bar and me. We stayed there for a couple of days. I wrote a letter to my parents and tried to describe what had happened, but I could not mention any names or places, of course. There were moments I could not get out of my mind, and I gave them some of the details. I said that bombing itself hadn't really worried me. "I thought one was fairly safe unless it was a direct hit, and then one doesn't need to worry anyway. That is just unlucky." I told them how the Jerrys used a queer sort of bomb that seemed to whistle all the way down to terrify people. I said: "It didn't terrify us, but it told us it was coming," and "I thought about what it means to come out alive when so many did not, but isn't it the same with any job in war?"

In the weeks that followed, there was nothing in the newspapers about the *Lancastria*. It was a month later that an article in the

Sunday Express included a full story and a photograph of the ship sinking. The loss was much worse than I had thought. An estimated 8,500 were on the ship and only 2,500 survived making it the worst naval disaster in British history. We guessed that the government had concealed the event from the public and we heard that when it happened, Churchill had said, "The newspapers have quite enough disaster for today." The other bad news was that on June 22, France had signed an armistice with Germany. Britain was now on its own.

While I was in France. Bar had been staying with Mary and Ted in Aldershot. Ted had gone over with the RCR to the Continent, but he had to return immediately as part of the evacuation. He got back safely but apparently arrived home wearing a sailor's outfit. I'm sure there was a story to tell about that, but I never knew it. I wondered if the sailor was now wearing Ted's army uniform.

My squadron had now moved to a base at Gatwick, south of London, and when I reported there, I was told to take a week's leave. I didn't feel I needed it; but it was required because of my recent experience. I thought this might be an ideal time to go to Stutton. After my short visit to see Aunt Isabel in April, I wanted to return with Bar to enjoy it together. She was keen on the idea, and we took the train to Ipswich in Suffolk. We loved exploring the grounds of the estate, the classic red-brick Stutton House and its gardens, lovely in the warm sunshine of late June. Tall Cedars of Lebanon with their huge branches provided shade beside the ponds in the heat of the day, and the Samoyed dogs made it feel like home. The town of Stutton is a small traditional English village with a couple of pubs, and is located on the River Stour, about eleven miles south of Ipswich. The surrounding area is mostly farming. The house and the estate are about two hundred acres of wooded park overlooking the river. My Aunt Isabel lived alone most of the time, but she loved having us to stay, and for as long as we wanted.

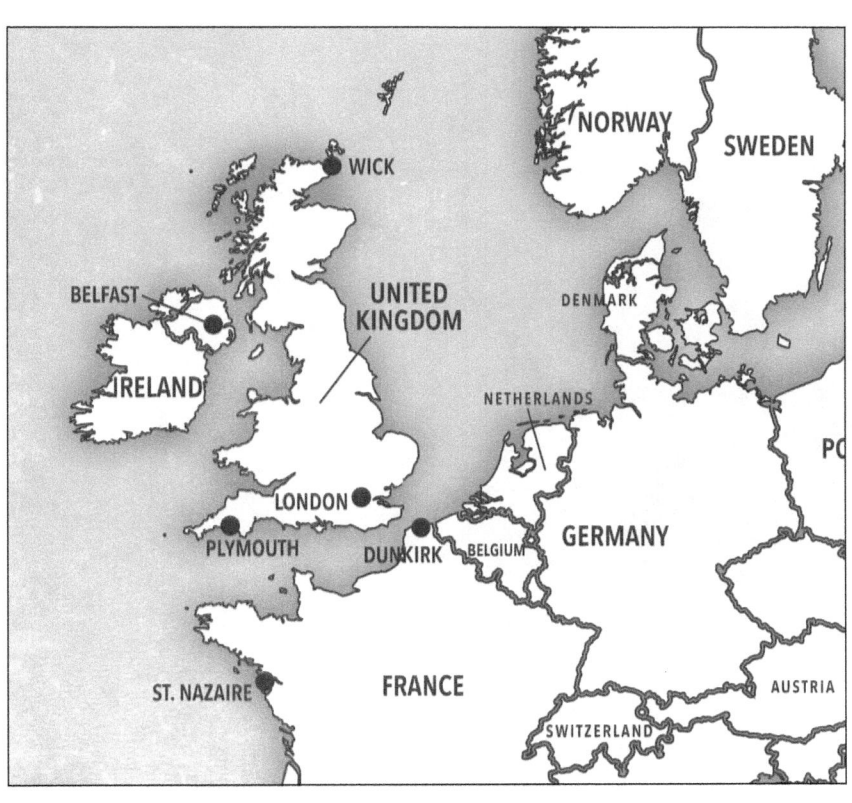

The gardens at Stutton, Suffolk, England, 1940.

ELEVEN

ENGLAND
Summer 1940

I returned to the RAF base at Gatwick after our restful week at Stutton. My squadron had suffered severe losses in France of both pilots and ground crew, many of them on the *Lancastria*. They were sort of camping on a base which didn't have all the usual facilities.

We knew the squadron was undergoing changes, but didn't know what they were or where we might be going next. It was summertime, lovely and warm, with days of almost cloudless skies. Bar was living nearby in Henley and Mary came to stay with her. Henley is on the main line to London, which made it easy for Bar and me to meet and spend a night at the Regent Palace Hotel, near Piccadilly Circus.

I went to Henley to see her whenever I wasn't on duty. We usually had tea together, or if there was time, went to the cinema. Once we took a bus to Reigate where I bought a model and made a balsa wood airplane that didn't fly very well. We were able to forget about the war and enjoy summer in England in these moments.

The Luftwaffe had been trying to bomb our shipping and seaports in order to shut off Britain's supplies and we expected an increase in bombing before Hitler would decide to invade. Reports in the papers told of German troop barges gathering in French ports to prepare for landings on England's coast.

I wondered how the RAF would respond and what role I might play. On July 20, the *London Daily Telegraph* reported that in a speech, Hitler had spoken to the British, saying, "One last appeal for Peace... War means an end for Britain or us." Churchill was defiant and responded, "The foulest thralldom that overhung mankind has sent its wholesome echoes through the world."

The United States described Hitler's words as "a masterpiece of hypocrisy and distortion." Britain was not going to trust Hitler.

The Germans increased their bombing at the end of July and into early August. Their raids on our shipping and ports like Plymouth and Bristol continued, but they were also now attacking our airfields to destroy our air defense. They were being met by RAF Spitfires and Hurricanes of fighter Command, who were dealing with the Luftwaffe very effectively.

Transportation was disrupted as railways were hit, making travel more difficult, but people went where they needed to go and got there as best they could. There were frequent articles in the newspapers about when and if Hitler would begin the invasion. Many expected it could happen soon. Would the Luftwaffe be able to get control of the air? At the time, RAF fighters were successfully holding them off, shooting down many of their aircraft. I was impressed by how confident people seemed about England's ability to defend itself and their seeming readiness to take Hitler on.

The *London Observer* quoted Duff Cooper, the Minister of Information, on August 18th saying that Britain was holding Hitler to his promise of invasion and would be "most disappointed" if he didn't show up. "We can assure him that he will meet with that welcome on our shores which no invader has ever missed."

Letters from home were very welcome and during the summer I received them often. Some of my family had arrived in Tadoussac: My aunt Mary and my grandfather told me who was there, when others were expected and how long they were staying – important information if you were spending the summer there yourself. Hearing this made me feel sad that I wasn't there too, but I knew it would be different because so many were away at war.

My grandfather wrote about his dog, Kara, one of the Samoyed pups my parents had bred. I wondered how he was getting along without my grandmother. I thought about the many times we had played golf together during my summers. He wrote that he had heard great things about what the RAF had been doing, although I doubt that he was hearing as much about our planes and pilots that were lost. He was aware of the imminent invasion by Germany, so I wrote back telling him that we were not afraid "In fact, we were rather waiting for Hitler to try it. We were feeling that he would get a little more than he expected because an Englishman will not give up his home without a fight; nor will a Canadian who has made England his home." His letters were always encouraging, and he said that, in his prayers, he remembered Bar and me. I knew what that meant to him, and it was also important to me. Letters from home were comforting, but their lives seemed so far away from what was happening here in Europe.

Bar and I were continually in touch with Mary and Ted. They were living close by, but we never knew when they might move or where Ted would be sent with his regiment. He wrote saying that his group of the RCR had been working very hard and that he hoped to be promoted to Captain. He was in the army, but somehow, he managed to go flying for about an hour and said he really enjoyed it. Ted had just received news that his older brother, Gilly Price, had been killed in an accident at the Price Brother's pulp mill in Chicoutimi, Quebec. I remembered Gilly from summers in Tadoussac; he was much older than us and I felt very badly for Ted.

I knew my squadron would get a new assignment any day now, and Ted suggested that, if I was away, Bar could come and stay with them. He said, "Don't worry about these Hampson girls; they really know how to look after themselves and I think they probably will stick together." Through the summer and early autumn Bar and Mary spent lots of time together while both Ted and I were away. They also worked as volunteers and, for a time, they stayed in the home of a widow and her family. When the sirens sounded, they were supposed to go to a nearby air-raid shelter. Instead, they chose the alternative of a mattress on the dining room floor. One night, Mary said "I can't see why we're sleeping here with that huge family portrait hanging over our heads. One distant bomb and it could land on us." So, they decided to return to their beds upstairs and "die in comfort."

By the middle of August, the Luftwaffe were hitting us almost everywhere. Hitler believed that if the Germans could destroy the RAF, he might persuade Britain to agree to a negotiated peace. The bombing was increasing, but the Luftwaffe had not yet bombed the large cities. Often as their aircraft were returning home, they unloaded their remaining bombs on the English countryside, killing civilians. The London papers covered the war on many fronts and in some detail. The reports of our daily aircraft losses were worrisome, but we were told that the Luftwaffe's losses were much greater and that we had shot down many more of their Heinkel 111's and Junker 88's. Our fighters, the Hurricanes and Spitfires, were defending Britain and were shooting down the enemy in large numbers. On August 15, we shot down 180 German aircraft, although later it was reported to be somewhat less. Day after day these reports were made in the press and on the BBC, and people followed them as they might follow a cricket test match.

At our base at Gatwick, we heard lots of rumors, and they tried to keep us informed through our briefings. Care was taken to avoid information that might be useful to the enemy, and we were constantly reminded not to talk in pubs. We were told that the RAF was running short of fighter pilots. Aircraft production had increased greatly, but Fighter Command needed to find pilots to fly them. You cannot train pilots overnight, so they were seeking pilots from both Bomber and Coastal Command. They were quite likely to choose pilots of single engine aircraft, like Fairey Battles. I hoped I wouldn't be selected. My preference was to remain in bombing.

The Battle of Britain continued and in late August, Churchill spoke about what RAF fighter pilots had done to defend Britain, saying, 'Never in the field of human conflict was so much owed by so many to so few." Bomber Command was doing its part as well, making successful raids on the Ruhr Valley and German industry. I wanted to be part of it all. Perhaps I was frustrated because our squadron was still re-organizing from its losses in France, and it had been almost two months since I had returned from the Continent. I had got to know the lads in our squadron better and we all hoped that we would hear soon where 98 Squadron would be going next.

On the night of August 24, London was bombed for the first time. The RAF retaliated immediately, and our bomber squadrons made raids on German industry and their sea bases in Hamburg, Ostend, Boulogne, and Dunkirk. They attacked Berlin with night-time raids and gave Hitler a dose of his own medicine, destroying Tempelhof airport, arms factories and scaring the population. We were ecstatic because the German people would now feel the reality of war.

In early September the Luftwaffe concentrated its raids on England's cities. Because our airfields were no longer the primary target, our fighter squadrons could be more easily launched against the Luftwaffe's large bombing formations as soon as they were identified by our radar systems. Hitler believed that death and destruction of our cities would destroy England's morale and bring it to its knees. He was wrong. London was hit day after day with heavy bombing which the newspapers covered in detail. The air raid sirens would sound, and sometimes the bombing would continue for more than five hours, day and night. We read that people were holding up under the strain of continuous night-time bombing, but it caused serious fatigue, and thus it was suggested that they should go to bed early. The bombing of London became known as the Blitz, and it continued for months. Fortunately, Bar and I were outside London, where the bombing was less concentrated. She was at home in Henley, and I was at my base in Gatwick. The Luftwaffe were bombing other cities and towns across England, and we read that they had hit and destroyed a church and several homes in Ipswich in Suffolk. This was very close to my family at Stutton.

The RAF increased its raids on Germany and on the occupied ports of Le Havre and Antwerp, and on German convoys. Because France was now occupied by the Germans, the RAF had to launch its raids from England and fly a greater distance to its targets in Germany, whereas the Luftwaffe could launch their raids from airfields in France, a much shorter distance to us. The longer distance meant that our fighters could give only limited protection to our bombers because fighters did not have the range to fly the whole distance and return. In addition, RAF fighters had a well-defined mission right now of defending England from daily bombing attacks. At the end of August, I was pleased to hear that No.1 Squadron of the Royal Canadian Air Force (RCAF) had arrived in England. They joined RAF Fighter Command.

Rivalry in the RAF between those who flew bombers and those who flew fighters was growing. We were called the Bomber Barons and they, the Fighter Glamour Boys. Pilots of the 1914-1918 War, like Billy Bishop, were famous and the aerobatics of the smaller single-seater planes had captured popular attention. When the fast fighters came into service, some young pilots were asked to be assigned to their squadrons. With their success these glamor boy fighters became famous. However, the bomber boys began to see them as cocky and self-important. They dressed in their white roll-neck sweaters, flapping scarves and flying boots. I received a letter from my father, who was full of admiration for the RAF fighters who were defending Britain. I wondered if he had been talking to an ex-fighter pilot and decided to tell him about the "friendly" and competitive rivalry between bomber and fighter airmen and what bomber crews sometimes thought of fighter pilots. I said: "we look upon them as rather glamorous boys while we bomber lads do the dirty work and are not heard of. Fighter pilots are a very snooty lot and are always showing off." I disagreed that if one can fly fighters one can fly anything. "They are easy to fly, they have lots of power and good control. They do what you want them to, which a bomber doesn't always. Unlike a bomber pilot, a fighter doesn't have to worry about his crew as well as himself. He is told where to go and how to get back and doesn't need to know navigation."

I also wanted to explain that "a fighter is armed with eight machine guns in front and has about six feet of solid engine between him and the enemy. And he is so fast no one can catch him." Bombers may carry bombs, but they have light armament. My father knew that bombers must fly long distances over enemy territory, but I pointed out that, "fighters never go far from home due to the small range of the aircraft."

Was he thinking that I might change my mind about flying bombers? I knew that choice was still possible. I thought about my training, the hard work, and the commitment it had taken. This and the dangers in flying may not have been recognized, but I enjoyed flying a bomber with a crew and I felt confident I could make a difference.

Fairey Battles en route to Iceland.

TWELVE

ICELAND
September 1940

We had been waiting to hear what would happen to 98 Squadron, where it would be sent, or even if it would continue as a bomber squadron. It was early September 1940 when the news came, and it was a big surprise. Probably the last place I would have guessed was Iceland. I knew where it was but very little about it.

Our squadron was given a preliminary briefing about Iceland and why it was so important. When Germany invaded and occupied Denmark and Norway in April, British forces had moved immediately to occupy Iceland. If Germany had got control, it would have gained a strategic advantage, enabling it to use Iceland as a base for its attacks on the Atlantic shipping routes that are vital to supplying Britain. German submarines and air patrols based in Iceland would be within easy range for attacks on Allied ships. Although Iceland is a neutral country, it has had a long relationship with Denmark and continues to share the same king. In early May, the Royal Marines had landed in Iceland, and in June, they were relieved by Canada's "Z" Force and three Canadian battalions of the Royal Regiment of Canada, Les Fusilliers de Mont-Royal and the Cameron Highlanders of Ottawa.

The Canadian "Z" Force constructed airfields, harbors, roads, bridges, defense positions and hospitals, including bases for naval and air patrols. We were told that the coastline of Iceland is over three thousand miles long with the Norwegian Sea on the east, and the Greenland Sea on the north. On its northwest is the two-hundred-mile Denmark Strait, which separates Iceland from Greenland, and to the south and west is the North Atlantic and the main convoy routes that supply Britain. We could never hope to patrol all this area, and our main role was to defend Iceland.

We were told that the aircraft flown by 98 Squadron were suitable for the role it would play in Iceland. The Fairey Battles had not performed well as bombers in France. To attack and destroy enemy ground forces on the move required low-flying bombing, mostly in daylight. Even when our fighters gave the Battles cover against Luftwaffe's Me109s attacking them, they were much slower and very vulnerable to German anti-aircraft flak. Many aircraft had been lost with pilots and crews and the squadron suffered further loss of airmen during the evacuation from France and the sinking of the *Lancastria*. We had heard rumors that the squadron might be disbanded altogether. I wondered where I might be assigned if this had happened. Now, 98 Squadron was being sent to Iceland to work with Coastal Command in occupying Iceland and patrolling the sea around it.

It is a very long way from Gatwick to Iceland and we had to fly our Fairey Battles there. To shorten the distance, we flew north to Wick, in Scotland, an airbase that was closest to Iceland. Wick is in the northernmost part of Scotland, north of Inverness, and on the coast. The airfield was built in 1939 as a base for Coastal Command. I flew my plane up there, hoping I was just turning it over to Coastal Command and that only a few of the squadron would have to go to Iceland. I was told to stay in Wick because all eighteen of 98 Squadron aircraft were going to Iceland.

Flying to Iceland would be difficult because of weather conditions. In these latitudes, unpredictable storm-force winds from the north or northwest can bring hail, rain, or snow and the risk of heavy icing. The westerly winds can make a trip longer and increase the risk of not having sufficient fuel to fly the distance. The Fairey

Battle had a range of 900 miles, and Iceland is about 750 miles from Wick. As pilots, we had to make an advanced assessment of winds at operational levels and plan the flight accurately to find our target. Unexpected headwinds could suddenly change the calculations, and if the weather closed in, there would be no alternative landing ground.

Wick was a prohibited area for security reasons. It's about fifty miles south of the Orkneys and Scapa Flow, where the Royal Navy had a base for the Home Fleet. It had already suffered several bombings during the past few months following the German occupation of Norway. I didn't know how long I would be staying in Wick, but I felt it would be at least several days and probably longer while waiting for favorable weather. I desperately wanted Bar to be with me, and I had no idea how long I might be away in Iceland. Thankfully, I was able to get a pass for her to come to be in Wick. Her trip north from London was quite challenging. The railways had been bombed, and to get to Wick by train, she had to spend a night under London's Euston station during an air raid. She was in the air-raid shelter with a large and very mixed group of people. She said they all had brought their British sense of humor with them. When she got on the train, it took several days and some unplanned changes before she finally arrived at Wick. I wondered how she could handle the trip with her pregnancy, but when I met her at the station, she said she was fine. We had a wonderful time exploring some of the north of Scotland in the cool autumn weather. We learned that Wick's name came from the Vikings and that St. Fergus was the patron saint. The surrounding countryside was muted and colorless. The houses were grey, and overcast skies made the sea and the shore look grey as well; and the wind blew constantly. The town was busy with fishermen, and the quays were filled with their boats when they returned from sea. We found a place to stay in Wick, but the usual policy meant that there were several nights I would have to remain on the base.

Bar and I had a very happy time together, but we knew it would end suddenly and with no warning. Then early one morning we were gone. Our squadron took off, and I had no chance to say goodbye to my Bar. I didn't know when I would see her again. It might be several months or more and I would have little or no news of her or where she was in England. I worried, knowing she was headed back south towards London as it was suffering the worst of the bombing.

The view of Iceland was certainly welcome after piloting a single-engine plane on a very long sea crossing. Our eighteen Fairey Battles now became part of Coastal Command, and we joined the combined air, sea, and ground forces that were defending Iceland and patrolling the large area around it. The country had been occupied since May. The Royal Navy was well established, and the Canadian "Z" Force had built defense positions and completed important infrastructure, including an aerodrome in Kaladarnes near Selfoss.

I never thought I would be stationed in a place like Iceland, but during a war, one can never know. I was still hoping that after flying an aircraft there, I would return to England for my next assignment and, hopefully, be nearer to Bar. However, they decided to keep me in Iceland with the squadron flying Fairey Battles, and I didn't know for how long. Bar would have left Wick and returned south. We heard that the bombing of London continued both day and night. I doubted that she was there, but I didn't know.

As part of Coastal Command, our flying consisted of shipping reconnaissance and patrols for U-boats that might threaten convoys on the North Atlantic. We were briefed about the convoys that would pass to our south and through the area known as the "Black Pit" between Halifax, Nova Scotia, and the mid-ocean meeting point. The "Black Pitt" had no air cover at all, and ships were most vulnerable to U-boat attacks. On September 22, the London Sunday paper, *The People,* reported that German Admiral

Raeder had advised Hitler that invading the Orkneys, Shetlands, Iceland, and Ireland had less risk than an invasion of Britain and, if successful, would enable the blockade of Britain. We were also warned that German battle cruisers might try to attack convoys by entering the North Atlantic from either the Norwegian Sea in the north or through the Denmark Strait. The *Scharnhorst* had sunk the *Rawalpindi* near the Faroe Islands last November and the aircraft carrier *Glorious* in June. Our Fairey Battles could provide some cover, but our range was limited; nonetheless, we were told to be on the lookout.

I learned a lot about Iceland. It is situated on the mid-Atlantic ridge between the geological plates of North America and Eurasia and lies on the southern edge of the Arctic Circle. By flying over and around it, I discovered very soon that its weather is an uncertain mix of horizontal rain, snow and ice, and high winds. It is also surrounded by dangerous seas that would be most unwelcoming if we ever had to ditch. We flew out of Kaldadarnes in the south of Iceland, but often, we flew into the small airstrips of Melgeroi near Reykjavik and Akureyri in the north. The hazards of flying were always present. Severe turbulence and cold were faced by all Coastal Command aircraft, which had to operate at low altitudes and had the ever-present risk of icing. It's not particularly healthy flying in the mountains and being bumpy, but it's all very beautiful and rather thrilling.

I had no idea how striking the volcanic mountains, snow-covered glaciers, and river valleys were, and by flying, I got to see them often. The colors were beautiful, especially when the sun was shining. The valleys have many shades of green; the volcanic mountains are brown, rust red, and purple, and the tops of volcanoes are capped by blankets of sparkling white snow glaciers that reach far towards the horizon. I never imagined a creation of anything like this, but it could all change in a minute with the weather. The glaciers that cover the mountains of volcanic rock melt into rivers, often grey in color because of the moraine, and become streams of cool, clear water. Geothermal heat from beneath the volcanic ground brings boiling water to the surface, sometimes in geyser spouts, and it supplies heat to parts of the population. Iceland is actively volcanic, and the central plateau, which covers most of the country, is erupting constantly, and earthquakes occur frequently throughout the year. It is a very large island surrounded by seas that can be ugly. Because it is at the Arctic Circle, the water is very cold, and so is the air. The shore is rugged but very beautiful, with green hills and snow-covered glaciers always in view. The people in Iceland had to be strong and independent to live in this demanding environment, which was far from the rest of the world and had a short growing season.

They imported much of their food and other essential supplies, except for fish. Because of the war, shipping had become uncertain, and prices for most things were increasing. Despite their hardship, I found people to be openly friendly and welcoming. Those who were hesitant had mixed feelings about us, depending on whether they considered us protectors or occupiers.

The lads in our squadron were a good bunch, and like me, they hadn't expected to find themselves in Iceland. Dick Shuttleworth was the only one I had known from before. He had joined the RAF when I did but had a few more flying hours. Shuttle was a delightful chap, over six-feet tall, with a bear-like presence, and was very likable. He had grown up in the north of England and had a Yorkshire accent. Like my father, his was also in the Army.

Our base near Kaldadarnes was more like a camp. We lived in tents, and it was damn cold. Thankfully, our mess was in a house, and we could get warm there. I had a little paraffin stove in my tent, which helped a bit, and I shared my tent with a Royal Army bloke who looked a bit like my brother-in-law, Johnny. It was a rather primitive life and quite damp and cold. The days in September were getting shorter, and this continued. I believe there would be only about five hours of daylight by winter. Our days were filled with flying operations when weather permitted. "Shuttle" and I flew together often, and we saw a lot of the country. He was a competent pilot, and I enjoyed being with him.

On the days we didn't fly, I found that I had time for my own thoughts, and I felt very far away from everyone who was important to me. I thought deeply about them and treasured the memories of our times together. I had faith that God would care for us, and I found comfort in this. I wrote letters to Bar and my family, even though I knew it would take a long time to reach them, and some letters might not get there, but I felt better when I wrote them. I told my parents where I was and what I was doing. I missed them both very much. In one letter, I tried to describe Iceland for them:

> *What Ho from the land of the midnight sun. I am learning quite a bit about this country. It is really very interesting. Did you know that many years ago, the Icelanders captured half of England, and people in the north of England used to speak Icelandic? Then they were driven out. The language has a distant resemblance to old English. Will you have a beer in Icelandic is "Will tu ave a piltzner." Everybody seems to speak English more or less. I went to Reykjavik the other day, pronounced "Reckyveek." The first syllable is accented, and the last is slurred. It is not a bad little town, but everything is very expensive. The people are quite well dressed, and the meals are described in English except for native dishes. The girls are very cold and won't look at a soldier or an airman. They all have blonde hair. Reykjavik is about the same size as one of those little towns between Toronto and Borden but not as big as Barrie. About one thousand years ago, the volcano, Hekla, erupted and wiped out half the island; then leprosy and the black death set in. There is still some leprosy on the island that is shut away. Iceland was once covered with birch trees, and*

about five hundred years ago, the largest trees were cut down, and an extra cold spell killed all the young saplings, leaving almost no trees on the island. However, the huge mountain ranges and the snowy peaks are rather grand. Hekla, the large volcano, last erupted in 1908, and they figure it is about two years overdue, even though it looks very peaceful. We have thought of stirring it up with a couple of bombs or something to cause a little excitement, but I somehow doubt we will. I don't think I can tell you much more about the island without giving away secrets, and I cannot do that, even if it is to you. I can't say that I love this place, but it is very interesting and well worth coming to. It is very cold, a sort of damp cold, invigorating and healthy, I expect, but I would love a nice easy chair in front of a fire to read in. When I was in Reykjavík, I had a hot bath at the main hotel. The only other wash I have had was a shower in the open the day after we got here. Of course, we have lots of water to wash your face and hands and to shave, but it's not very hot. This may be my own fault if I would get up when my Batman brought it in the mornings. We have seen Okjocull, which is the largest glacier in Europe, and I was able to see one of the geysers erupt but didn't get to swim in one. There are hot springs on the island, and it looks extraordinary to see a stream flowing along with steam coming off it and to feel the warmth from it. It is also a great saving on fuel for heating in some places because they use it for hot water and for their radiators. There is plenty of game on the Island – snipe, golden plover, duck, and swan. It is meant to be protected, but our food supply comes first. The natives don't seem to worry much about it.

I also asked my parents if, when I returned to England, they might send me a tin of Piccadilly pipe tobacco. Strangely, we couldn't get it in England. In Iceland, we could get some things at cost through the NAAFI, the Navy, Army, Airforce, Institutes.

One evening, a week or two after our arrival, we had cocktails with the Canadians. There was a lad named Savoy from Montreal who gave me four packs of Sweet Caporal cigarettes, which was very nice of him. He also offered me a piece of *sucre la crème*. It was awfully good and what we used to have after lunch during summers in Tadoussac. I had a conversation with two Canadian Officers, Major LeClair from the Montreal Militia and Lt. Col. Grenier, their Commanding Officer. They said they had known my father in 1937 when he was a District Officer in Command in Montreal.

Letters from my parents took about six weeks to reach me. I had told them that Bar was pregnant and said that if it's a boy, we would call him Michael. They asked when Bar expected "Michael" to arrive, and I replied, "Probably about the beginning of February." That would be a little more than nine months from when we were married. Thinking ahead to Christmas, I said that it didn't make much sense for us to send presents. I felt sorry that we weren't closer and told them that when the war was over, we would get together. Either we would come to Canada, or they could come over to England, where they might like to show me their old haunts.

Writing about the war, I said that I thought Germany was getting worried. Hitler had called the RAF "pirates of the air," a sure sign of a loser who starts to curse his opponents. I felt there wasn't much doubt we had stopped the avalanche of attacks, that it was now up to us to build and replace the ruins, and that, with the British spirit, we could do it. I also told my parents that I had just received a letter from the Royal Humane Society saying that I had been awarded their medal for valor. I supposed it was because of what I had done to save the woman off the *Lancastria*.

I always felt comfortable telling my parents about my career and how I was doing. In one of my letters, I wrote this about the RAF:

I hope after the War, the inferiority of the RAF, by having no tradition, will be wiped out. I think it's making a fair name for itself. Not that I'm doing much towards it, but we can't all be in the limelight, can we? I expect everyone will have his turn sooner or later. We heard a recording of the King's speech yesterday. And it was very good, I thought. He seems to speak better every time.

I had been in Iceland for a month and a half now, and it was almost the end of October. We heard news that the heavy bombing on England continued but that the Luftwaffe was suffering huge losses, and that Hitler might decide not to launch his planned invasion. On the North Atlantic, German U-boats were sinking merchant ships and threatening the supply of armaments and food that were so important to Britain.

We hoped that the United States would soon agree to provide more help. On the positive side, we heard that Greece had entered the war and was giving the Italians their due after Italy had invaded Albania. At times, I felt frustrated being in Iceland when so much was happening elsewhere. The RAF was involved in many parts of the war, and I wanted to play a meaningful role. I hoped to be back in England by Christmas to be with Bar.

Everyone in our squadron worried about the bombing in England. We didn't know what might be happening to our wives, girlfriends, and families. We had short-wave wireless that gave us the BBC but nothing else. I wrote to Bar, c/o the Bank of Montreal in London. I didn't know how she was or how she might be feeling now that she was almost six months pregnant. I was confident that she could handle most things, but these were not normal times. I assumed that she was somewhere in the south of England, but I hoped she was not in a dangerous spot.

Bar's letters to me often seemed to go missing. They took at least two weeks to reach me when they did. I was relieved that she hadn't mentioned being in or near London. She had been staying in Suffolk at Stutton and said that Gwen was perfectly sweet to her and did anything for her. That was just like Gwen, but she said that Aunt Isabel was looking very tired under the strain. She is not young. It helped to think that if one puts one's trust in God, it is in pretty safekeeping.

One evening, I saw one of the Canadians who told me his division was being re-assigned to join the rest of the Royal Canadian Regiment in England. They had been in Iceland since the summer, and apparently, a troop ship was to take them sometime around the end of the month. Almost concurrently, I was informed, along with some others on 98 Squadron, that I was to leave Iceland and report to Bomber Command in England, where I would be reassigned to another squadron. We would be sailing on the troop ship with the Canadians. I was very pleased as this meant that I might be with Bar again very soon.

However, bad news followed. On October 28, the *Empress of Britain* was sunk off the coast of Ireland. I felt that I knew her well because she had made regular crossings between London and Quebec City, and during my summers in Tadoussac, I saw this beautiful white ship passing by on the St Lawrence River. She had brought the King and Queen back to England after their visit to Canada in 1939. When the war began, she was painted grey and used as a troop ship to bring many Canadian troops over to the War. An older ship of 40,000 GRT, she was the largest in the Canadian Pacific passenger fleet. Her loss may not have been that serious for Canadian Pacific, but it brought the realities of war close to home.

On October 30, we boarded a grey troopship and departed from Iceland. She was the RMS *Antonia*, a rather old Cunard steamship, smaller than the *Lancastria*, and quite comfortable until we encountered rough seas, but most important, she was headed for England. While on board, we made the best of it all with the chaps from the 2nd Canadian Division. I joined the Canadians for lunch one day and for dinner the next evening. I knew of Col. Headley Basher, of the "Z" Force, and others in that unit, such as John Hansen, who had been an usher at Jean and Johnny's wedding. Many of them asked after my father. We invited them to our cocktail party, and Brigadier Frank Page, who led the Canadian "Z" Force, also attended. When I talked with him, he said he would look up my sister in England as he was going to be near where she had been living; I hoped she was still there.

We encountered some rough weather, and for a day, the skies were dark and grey. The North Atlantic is cold in October. I didn't feel well, but I stayed active. We had a concert one evening, and I was the master of ceremonies. It was quite fun. One afternoon, I was sitting with two chaps drinking a bottle of Molson's Export ale when they described how they were at sea for nine days in an open boat after their merchant ship had been torpedoed by a U-boat. It was apparently very rough, and the German submarine surfaced, came alongside, and asked if they had enough food. They said, "Yes, thank you," and the sub left. I was sure my brother Ronnie would enjoy this story, and I wrote about it in a letter to him.

Back in England, it was wonderful to be with Bar again. She looked healthy while showing visible signs of pregnancy. I don't think the rationing was a problem. She hadn't lost any weight. Perhaps moving around wasn't as easy for her, but she looked very happy, even glowing, a contrast to everything else that seemed grey. We had so much to tell each other that couldn't be said in letters. She described how stoic the English were and how they kept their sense of humor during the heavy bombing in September and October. She had moved about, spending time with her sister Mary, who was also expecting, as was my sister Jean. Bar was such a good sport. Thank goodness for the times she was able to go to Stutton. She had told me in her letters how much she loved it and that she had done volunteer work in the community. Stutton is well away from the cities and safer from the bombing, except when the Luftwaffe bombers dump their unused bombs over Suffolk on their route home.

It was the first week of November, and I hadn't been back for more than a couple of days when I received word of my next assignment. I would be leaving 98 Squadron to join 88 Squadron. This might have been good news until I heard that my new squadron was in Northern Ireland, outside Belfast. I had just spent six weeks in Iceland, and now the RAF wanted me to go to Northern Ireland. Why didn't they want me in England, where I was more likely to be flying bombing raids over the continent? What about Bar? We had been married only six months, and I felt I had hardly been with her. I knew it was hard for her to be alone and for us to be apart. Northern Ireland is a long way, and she was not happy that I was being sent away from England again.

My new squadron had seen extensive operations in France during May and had also experienced heavy losses. When the squadron returned to England in June, it was assigned to RAF Sydenham, a base near Belfast, and its role was to carry out patrol duties over the Western Approaches. When I joined the squadron, I hoped to fly something other than Fairey Battles. There were now several newer aircraft or upgrades. Unfortunately, 88 Squadron was flying mostly Battles, the same aircraft I had been flying in Iceland. The Fairey Battles have limited defenses, with one 303 Browning machine gun mounted on the starboard wing. They were now used mainly in Coastal Command to patrol the shipping routes and for coastal defense. I wasn't sure what was in store for me, but I was ready for the experience.

Some of the lads in Jimmy's squadron.

THIRTEEN

NORTHERN IRELAND
November 1940

Northern Ireland was cloudy and wet, and the days seemed very dark. I arrived at the RAF Coastal Command base in Sydenham in early November when daylight hours were short. It reminded me a bit of November in Canada, but Ireland is farther north, and the days were almost two hours shorter. While I was quite interested in knowing more about Northern Ireland, I would much rather have been in England with Bar.

There were numerous air bases because it was the most westerly launching point for aircraft to protect incoming convoys. 88 Squadron base at Sydenham had been completed only a few years ago and was located a few miles from Belfast. Our squadron was now part of Coastal Command's defenses of Northern Ireland and what was known as the "Western Approaches", the area to the immediate west of Ireland and Britain. This geography and our role were explained to us shortly after I arrived. We were to help protect a key part of the lifeline to Britain. Because the port cities on Britain's east and south coasts from Aberdeen to Plymouth had been bombed and were closely watched by enemy submarines, the ports in the north and west were now vital for receiving supplies of armaments, food, oil, and other goods that were crossing the North Atlantic.

Our squadron was to search and patrol the sea lanes leading into these ports. Convoys of ships crossing the Atlantic arrived on the Western Approaches and entered the North Channel into the Irish Sea to the ports of Belfast, Greenock on the River Clyde, and Liverpool to the south. It was stressed that their safe arrival depended on us in Coastal Command. Our patrols out over the sea were limited by the range of our aircraft, and we focused mainly on the area around Northern Ireland, the North Channel, and the Irish Sea. The Fairey Battle had too short a range for effective operations against German U-boats on the Atlantic and could not carry the heavy depth charges that would be needed to sink a submarine.

Other squadrons, 209 and 240, had longer-range aircraft, Sunderlands and Consolidated Catalinas, capable of defending convoys and searching for U-boats. All the RAF squadrons based around Belfast were involved in another role: to work with the Army in the event that Hitler decided to invade Ireland.

November was a difficult month. I felt alone and somewhat discouraged. I wondered why I was here after being away in Iceland when others with the same or less training were flying over the Channel and dropping bombs on the enemy. That is what I wanted to do. I began to think ahead about Christmas, and although it was still a way off, I wrote letters home, knowing they would take a while to get there. I found that writing was helpful. Bar would stay in England because she was expecting, and I wondered when the baby would arrive. We knew it might be in December because that would be nine months from when she became pregnant. I had told my parents that it would be sometime in February, so we would have to say the baby was born prematurely. We didn't know when we would see each other again or whether I could get leave over Christmas. I thought about what it would be like to be a father. I tried to imagine how my father and my grandfather had felt when they were in my situation.

I wrote more letters. One was to my dear Godmother, Aunt Evelyn, in Sackville, New Brunswick, to wish her a Merry

Christmas. Her daughter Ann was somewhere in England, and I wanted to get in touch. I knew Ann in Quebec City when she used to visit her grandparents, the Merediths. I told my aunt what it was like to be in England, that I thought the English were wonderful, and how tremendously helpful and generous they were to each other, even when they had lost everything themselves. I said that the blackouts were a nuisance. I wondered how people in Canada felt when they were so far away from it all. Possibly, it was worse than being in England, where everybody seemed busy and usually cheerful, even when they were being bombed out of house and home.

I had just received a letter from my father saying that he had recently been flying with oxygen. He had flown over the Canadian Rocky Mountains to the west coast to take up a new posting as Major General of Pacific Command with responsibility for Alberta and British Columbia, and his headquarters were in Victoria, B.C. Flying with oxygen was an entirely new experience for him. In my letter, I said, "It sounds like quite a trip. Of course, we wear oxygen masks over 15,000 ft., but it's part of the job with us. I think it would be quite different traveling on a passenger plane." My mother and Ronnie will join my father there in December, so I wished them all a Happy Christmas.

It took me a little while, but when I settled into Sydenham with my new squadron, I began to enjoy the lads I worked with. Many had wives or girlfriends, and I thought Bar would enjoy them if she could come over here. Dick Shuttleworth had been promoted recently to Flight Lieutenant and was now with 226 Squadron. He had an Irish girlfriend. Jack Meakin and his wife Betty were a couple that I knew Bar would enjoy meeting. Jack was a couple of years older than me and had some operations experience flying Blenheims. We frequently flew together and enjoyed some fun on our time off. Belfast is a collection of separate villages, and the people in them are somewhat isolated and occupied with their work, their churches, and their communities. However, there was a large wartime population of Naval, Army, and RAF personnel stationed in and around the city, and this was reflected in the gaiety of its nightlife. There was a good choice of theaters and cinemas that we sometimes went to. The harbor was filled with navy and supply ships being refitted or repaired at Harland and Wolff, the company that built so many ships, including the *Titanic*.

Short Brothers built aircraft, and with other industries, they employed hundreds of workers in the city. Outside of Belfast, there are farms, and Northern Ireland is a major producer of food for the rest of England, especially milk and vegetables. The countryside is very green and ideal for golf. I managed to play a couple of times with the lads, but you had to share the fairways with grazing cattle or roaming sheep, and usually some wind and rain. The country was very nice, but I wished it wasn't so damp. One had a hard time keeping dry.

The weather was a major challenge and often impossible for us to fly. It was also a reason for many flying accidents where pilots and airmen were killed. Flying through a storm can be exciting, even if not recommended. Once, in a thunderstorm, when a streak of lightning went past us, my wireless operator said, "Sir, did you see that? I'm reeling in my aerial."

Weather was the worst problem for us, but it was just as much a problem for Jerry. Every pilot wants to fly to gain experience, and when nothing else is known about him, he is judged on the number of hours he has flown. I was flying more now, and my work was more interesting, but otherwise, things seemed very quiet. We weren't being bombed, and the war seemed far away. Thankfully, the flying kept us focused on improving our ability and learning from experience.

News about the war was more encouraging. We heard that our troops in Egypt were putting on a grand show and had driven Italian forces back into Libya. In my letter to my father, I told him that the Army in England was beginning to hold their heads up again after their losses in France in May. I knew he would want to hear this. About my squadron, I said:

> *I can't tell you its number, of course, but I like it very much and have come to know the lads much better. They are young, mostly about my age, and I enjoy being with them. Many joined up because of the war. Had it been peacetime, they would have likely become barristers, teachers, bankers, or businessmen. They are educated, well trained, capable of flying aircraft or as airmen, meeting other demands on them, and they are very committed. They took what they were doing seriously but were ready for fun, practical jokes on each other, and good laughs in the mess.*

I told him that two of my friends had more flying hours than me, but we shared some good times together in the squadron and during our time off. We had all been flying Battles for some time and agreed we had enough of them. We had heard that we might soon be flying the Blenheim aircraft instead.

Jimmy holding Michael.

FOURTEEN

SUFFOLK
December 1940

December came, and the weather turned colder. On the morning of December 9, I received a telegram from my cousin, Gwen, in Suffolk. Bar had given birth to a baby boy very early that morning. She was in Bury St. Edmunds, about thirty-five miles north of Stutton. We had already chosen his name: Michael. Both were doing well. I completed my flight patrol that day in a bit of a daze. I'm sure that if Jerry had come along, I would never have noticed him. Of course, I wanted to get over to see Bar and my son, but I couldn't get a flight back to England. It is a long trip over from Northern Ireland, about 450 miles, so I wired back and forth frantically for a day or two. The squadron suggested that I wait until my leave began on December 16. However, on the 15th, I got a space on a Lockheed Hudson over to London, and that evening, I got up to Bury St. Edmunds to be with Bar and Michael. Bar was in a small nursing home where Michael had been born during an air raid. She was very comfortable. The matron had taken them both under her wing and was treating them like family. I was able to finally hold my son in my arms. I'm not sure what I expected to feel, but it was wonderful. I was holding a living thing, a brand new life that I had helped create. He was mine and I was his father.

I found a room at the Everards Hotel, about five minutes away. It was hardly luxurious, but the hotel was quite historic, being located near the marketplace, the old wool hall, and the corn exchange. We had a wonderful Christmas together. Bar said it was the happiest she could remember. We had so much to talk and laugh about, and in the evenings, we would often read to each other. She told me that one day, about a week before Michael was born, she had been walking along the main street in the town of Ipswich when a German Messerschmidt flew down, machine-gunning as it went. She said she could see the pilot's face as he flew by and thought it was a "pretty cheeky thing to do." She managed to take shelter in a covered doorway.

Our time together was always so short, and I was fortunate to be able to get two weeks leave, but by New Year's Eve, I was back with my squadron at Sydenham. I spent the evening with "Shuttle," Dick Shuttleworth, and his friend Jolly, and Alan and Betty Lynn. Alan was from South Africa. Together, we saw the New Year. On New Year's Day, I went to a very good concert with friends, and we all gathered in the mess afterward. I wrote a letter to Bar that evening. She and Michael had to stay in England until I found a place for us to live, and we could arrange for them to come over to Belfast. I had made inquiries among the chaps in the squadron who were married. Some had rented small houses not far from the base.

Suffolk 181

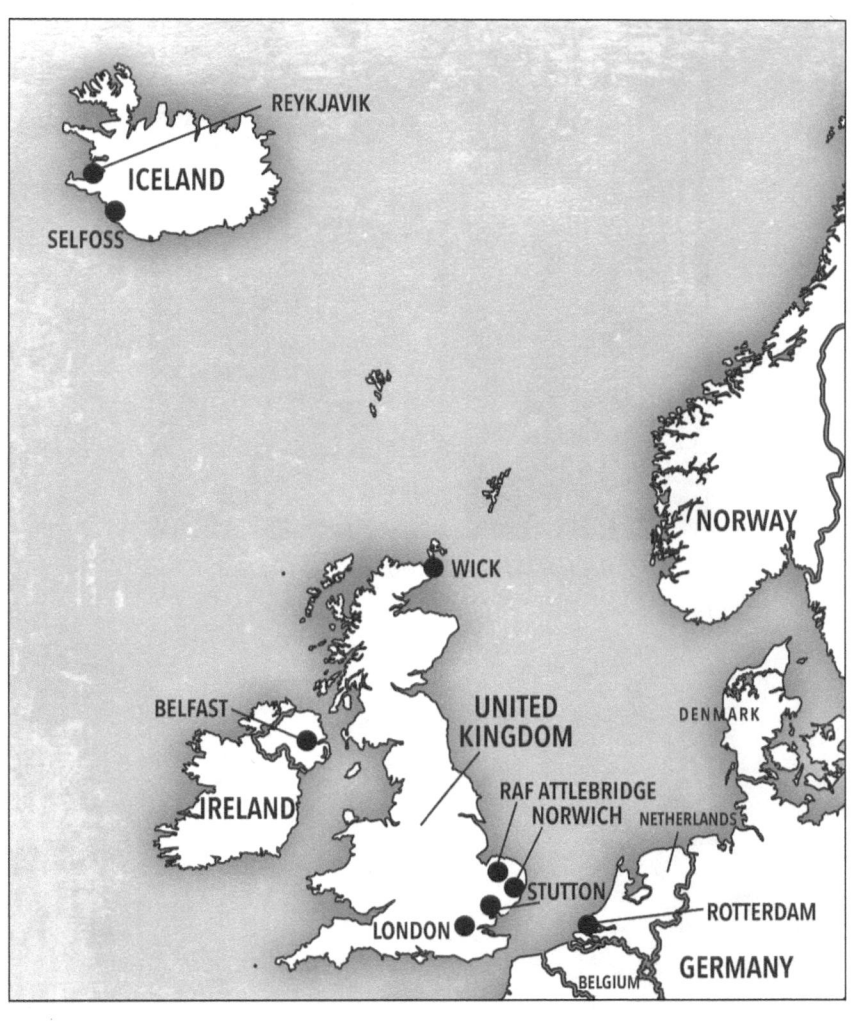

Bridget, Micheal's Irish nanny, 1941.

Jimmy with Michael in the pram.

FIFTEEN

BELFAST
Winter 1941

January was very cold and dark. The days were short, and on some mornings, there was even snow on the ground. Storms or fog rolling in from the coast meant we were often unable to fly. Although our newer pilots were learning and anxious to become involved, their lack of experience increased the risk and frequency of mishaps, especially in poor weather. One morning, I attended a funeral for a fighter pilot who was killed in a landing accident and that kept me from flying. Another day I had to attend a court-martial. Sometimes I had to take my turn as "orderly officer" in charge of security on the base. However, weather was the usual reason we were unable to fly and when I was on "immediate," meaning ready to fly, I was very often frustrated by poor weather.

One morning, one of my mates, Jack Rose, flew me over to Montrose Airbase in Scotland in the back of his Battle. Montrose is north of Edinburgh on the shore of the North Sea. There was lots of snow up there, and I was supposed to pick up an aircraft and fly it back. Jack said we could look forward to a nice warm stopover in the officer's mess, but we arrived to find the mess had been blown up. Montrose had been bombed since the last time I had been there, and the mess and other buildings had been destroyed. Nor was my aircraft ready, so I came back the same way, cramped and uncomfortable in the back of the cockpit.

It was very cold, and I gave Jack some good-natured grief about it. Exploits like this gave us a break from other days, which could sometimes be pretty dull. Bombing practice was now an active part of our training, but it didn't last long, and our flying time was often short. Our patrols took us in many directions. I flew over to Rathlin Island off the North coast of Ireland. Some days, we did photography, but the January weather continued to be frustrating.

On Sundays, I attended church whenever I could. During the evenings, we went to the movies or sometimes to concerts or plays. I saw a movie called *The Sea Hawk*, starring Errol Flynn as an English Privateer defending his queen and country against the Spanish Armada. I enjoyed the combination of history and adventure. On another day, I had tea with Alan and Betty Lynn, and that evening, we went to see Charlie Chaplin in *The Great Dictator*. What an amazing performance. I loved it, especially the way Chaplin played both Hitler, the dictator, and the persecuted Jewish barber.

Our Squadron's job of patrolling the coasts took us eastward, towards the Isle of Man, and between Giant's Causeway in the north and Carlingford Lough in the south. One morning, I flew out over the North Channel. There was good visibility, and I saw three convoys with destroyer escorts. I flew over them, but I was challenged about eight times by a patrolling Blenheim. To take a more direct route to the Atlantic Ocean on the west, one would have to fly over Eire, a neutral country. We were told that the United States, also being neutral, had put pressure on Eire to open a flight path directly to the West Coast. This was called the "Donegal Air Corridor."

Bar's birthday was January 21. She would be twenty-two, and I had bought a birthday present to send to her. Things seemed more hopeful that she and Michael would be able to come over to Ireland soon. My friends helped us to look for a small house, and Bar tried to find some help for Michael when they arrived. In her letters, she said she felt lucky not to be in the cities where the bombing continued nightly. She had been staying with her sister while Ted was away and said that transportation was seriously disrupted and that driving during blackouts was very dangerous. Rationing of food made things difficult, but she was able to get an egg once a week for Michael. She had a bicycle, but she was not able to use it much with Michael. I felt so bad that she was alone. There had been a measles outbreak around Stutton, so she was not able to be there with Michael and had been staying at Miss Read's, who apparently is known as Peggy of Grove Hall. It was a boarding house of some kind. she said that Michael got the measles anyway, but it was a mild case.

The threat of Hitler's invasion was still on people's minds. The newspapers were full of articles on the possible timing, and opinions on German strategies. The RAF had destroyed some of Hitler's preparations by bombing the landing barges in French ports, yet some felt an invasion could still happen sometime this year. German bombing raids continued at night, and our nighttime fighters were having difficulty putting up an effective defense. We read about the heavy bombing of Coventry, Manchester and Sheffield. These industrial centers and the port cities of Bristol, Cardiff, Plymouth, and Southampton were being badly hit. RAF bombing squadrons based in the south and east of England were now bombing Berlin and the Ruhr Valley. We were amused by a comment from the Air Minister, Sir Archibald Sinclair, who said that the RAF was "the most glorious and happy band of men who have ever gone to war together." Those of us at RAF Sydenham in Northern Ireland would have been happier if we were closer to the action. We knew we were ready. 88 Squadron had good aircrews, and we knew we could depend on each member to do his part.

At the end of January, Bar and Michael arrived in Northern Ireland. I was so excited to see them. We had a small house in east Belfast on the outskirts of the city and closer to the air base at Sydenham. Through friends, we also found someone to help us to look after Michael. Her name was Bridget, and with her Irish lilt, she was a delight. She loved Michael and even made him a circus of animals – a giraffe, elephant, lion, antelope, hippo, and bear, all in different bright colors and ready to hang on our tree next Christmas. I think Bar found Ireland very cold, damp, and dark; however, having Bridget to help meant she was able to get out and meet people. She soon got to know the wives and girlfriends of my friends. When we were off duty, we played bridge together some evenings. It was a happy time, and we were all ready to help each other when needed.

In February, our squadron received some Blenheim aircraft. Unlike the Battle, the Blenheim was a twin-engine aircraft. It was designed as a light bomber, but it had undergone important improvements. The Blenheim Mark IV was fitted with protective armor, and its nose was extended. It was powered by two 905 hp. Bristol Mercury radial piston engines and armed with a .303 Browning machine gun in the port wing, two .303 guns in the dorsal turret and two more mounted under the nose. It could carry a 1,000 lb. bomb load internally. Although it had two engines, it was not much larger than the Battle, but it had a longer range of over 1,400 miles and a slightly greater cruising speed of 198 mph. I wasn't sure just when I would get to fly one, but I hoped it would be soon.

On February 9, Bar heard the exciting news that her sister had given birth to a son. We now had a nephew and Michael, a first cousin his age. Mary and Ted decided to call him Greville after Mary and Bar's father. The month of February moved into March, the sun shone, and the days got longer and warmer. The heavy bombing of cities in England continued, and Liverpool was badly damaged. On March 13 and 15, Glasgow suffered an all-night blitz. The *Glasgow Daily Record and Mail* described the Nazi guiding policy of indiscriminate bombing of both civilian homes and shipbuilding on Clydeside. The damage and loss of life was extensive. The Prime Minister promised that "for every bomb the Germans drop on us, we shall presently drop four on them." We read the newspapers as often as we could, and while we focused daily on our flying patrols and training, we frequently discussed what we were hearing about the war. There were calls for more aggressive RAF tactics and raids on German submarine factories and invasion ports. The Luftwaffe were continuing heavy night bombing, and their raids were now being carried out further north. Belfast's shipyards and aircraft industry were certainly in their range. Our fighters, Hurricanes and Spitfires, had handed the Germans heavy losses, but the Luftwaffe's night-time raids were still getting through. We knew that convoys crossing the Atlantic with vital supplies were losing ships to U-boat attacks at an alarming rate. Perhaps the only encouraging news was that in March, something called "Lend Lease" had been passed by the US Congress. We weren't sure what this would mean, but we hoped the United States would send more support. We really wanted them to declare war on Germany.

Jimmy and Michael at Stutton.

SIXTEEN

ENGLAND
April 1941

I was due for some leave in April, and Bar and I wanted to return to England for the Easter holidays. We would have Michael with us, and it would be a good chance to see friends and family again, and we could spend some time relaxing at Stutton. On March 28, we received more exciting news. This time, it was my sister, Jean, who gave birth to a son. They called him Ronald, after my father. Apparently, he was born in a military hospital, which created considerable interest, including a visit from the Duke of Kent.

During our leave in England, we visited Mary and Ted, as well as Jean and Johnny. Lots of photos were taken of us all together holding our sons, three cousins of the same age. It was wonderful to be with them again as a family and as very good friends. England was looking beautiful. Signs of spring were showing, and it was so nice to be able to enjoy this beautiful country, even while a war was raging.

Back in January, the Luftwaffe had bombed Dublin. This was a surprise, and we thought it must be a mistake because Eire was a neutral country. There was damage, but no one was killed. Some guessed that a few German aircraft had messed up on their navigation and mistaken Dublin for one of the cities in England. This made little sense because Dublin is almost 150 miles from Liverpool or Manchester across the Irish Sea. We thought Germany would want to stay on good terms with Eire, hoping it might act as an obstacle for Britain or even become a German ally. A more worrying thought was that the Luftwaffe pathfinders might have been headed for Belfast and had hit Dublin instead.

Then it happened. In early April, while we were still in England, the newspapers reported a bombing raid on Belfast. We learned that on April 7 and 8, the Luftwaffe staged an attack on the dockyards and did considerable damage to Short Brothers, where the Stirling bomber was made. The Short Sunderland aircraft was being used against the U-boats on the North Atlantic. Further bombing raids seemed quite likely. On Easter Monday and Tuesday, April 14 and 15, the Luftwaffe delivered a terrible blitz on Belfast. We read in *the London Daily Telegraph* that they had dropped incendiary bombs on residential and shopping areas, followed by high-explosive bombs. The *Telegraph* described it as indiscriminate destruction of homes, including churches and hospitals. The shipyards were heavily damaged along with Harland and Wolff, who built destroyers, aircraft carriers, and mine sweepers and repaired other ships damaged during the war. Many nearby homes of dockyard workers were destroyed.

Belfast had the highest population density of any city in Britain. It was not adequately prepared with anti-aircraft defenses and air-raid shelters. RAF Fighter Command had only a few fighter squadrons to stage an effective defense in the air. Belfast had assumed that it was far enough north and beyond the range of the Luftwaffe. This might have been true until Germany took over airfields in France that were much closer to Britain. More than a thousand people were killed, thousands more were injured, and many lost their homes. What was amazing was that, within a few hours, the firemen of Dublin and other towns in the south of Ireland arrived to assist their Belfast colleagues in the rescue.

Later, we read in *The Irish Times* that:

> *Humanity knows no borders, no politics, no differences of religious belief. Yesterday, for once, the people of Ireland were united under the shadow of a national blow. The hand of good fellowship was reached across the border. Men from the South worked with men from the North in the universal cause of the relief of suffering.*

We were very happy to still be in England, and before leaving, we were able to stay at Stutton House again for a few days. My uncle, Tim Alexander, was also there, and he gave me the pocket Royal Services Diary, made of leather and full of information about the Services. I resolved to write in it daily. The weather was sunny and cool, and we walked the beautiful grounds beside the lake. My leave was coming to an end with a cocktail party on our last night. Bar, Michael, and I set off by train the next morning to be with Jean for Ronnie's Christening. It was May 4, our first wedding anniversary, and it was nice to celebrate it with them.

Belfast Blitz 1941.

SEVENTEEN

BELFAST
Spring 1941

The following morning, we returned to Belfast and arrived quite unprepared for what we found. Our little home was a pile of rubble. Another raid on Belfast had taken place on the evening and morning of the May 4 and 5, and the night of May 5 and 6. Once again, the Luftwaffe had dropped incendiary and high-explosive bombs, including land mines attached to parachutes. The center of Belfast and the historic Royal Avenue were hit badly and, as we were to discover, the residential areas in East Belfast were also destroyed.

We managed to salvage a few things from the wreckage of our home, and we were fortunate to be able to stay with Jack and Betty Meakin until we found another house. One can feel overcome by a certain numbness when so many tragedies are happening around you. The situation we witnessed in Belfast after the bombing was awful. So many people were killed, wounded, or without homes as whole neighborhoods had been destroyed. There was no choice but to keep going. Bar and I recovered, and Michael smiled happily in his large English pram. We were fortunate to have friends who helped us.

The month of June was full of family birthdays. I would be twenty-three. I wrote to my mother, whose birthday was June 3, the same as my own. Then I wrote to my grandfather and to Bar's mother, Mrs. Hampson, whose birthday was June 4. It was also the same as my goddaughter, Sheila, who was now 4 years old. They all seemed so far away. We continued to live, not knowing what each day might bring. Bar and I had a social life that pretty much centered around those we knew on the base. Bar had met Betty Meakin when she arrived in February, and they had seen each other often.

Betty's husband, Jack, was an experienced pilot, and we often flew together. We enjoyed our evenings, sometimes with Betty and Jack, for supper, playing bridge, or a trip nearby to get seafood, such as cockles. In the mornings, I usually had to be up before dawn for a 5 A.M. take-off. Bar was able to carry on some meaningful friendships during the day with the wives she had come to know on the base. Sometimes Michael was included, but Bridget was often there to look after him if Bar wanted to get out on her own. When I returned from an exercise, I would often shoot up over the house to let Bar know I was on my way home. There were some lovely roses growing around the house, so I had time to give them some attention. Bar was not very interested in gardening, but I enjoyed it, and I liked growing vegetables.

On the days we weren't flying, there were frequent cricket matches on the base. I wasn't very good. I might make a catch, but I didn't bowl, and I was usually put out without scoring. They call this a "duck," and a "double duck" is when you are put out in both innings without scoring. Some of the lads were very good at the game and seemed very patient with my inadequate performance on our team.

Our flying soon had the benefit of better weather and longer days, and I was more active doing tactical exercises, usually two flights each day. We had been told that on May 27, one of 209 Squadron's Catalina flying boats had sighted the German battleship *Bismarck* and re-established contact for the Royal Navy. The *Bismarck* had sunk the British battle cruiser H.M.S. *Hood* and was being pursued by the British Fleet, but contact had been lost. The Catalina has a very long range and was commanded by F/O Dennis Briggs, flying from the squadron's base at Castle Archdale on Lough Erne.

This helped to remind us how important our role was in patrolling the Western Approaches, but many of us felt we were missing the real action flying bombers. We knew that Bomber Command was using Blenheims on enemy raids from bases in England, most likely from East Anglia. The next day, after the usual tactical exercises, I flew a Tiger Moth over to the base at Aldergrove in County Antrim to fly a Blenheim Mark 1 back. It took twenty minutes.

The squadron began to receive more Blenheims, and our flying operations were transferred to them. Its crew of three included a pilot, an observer, and a gunner. The pilot flew the plane, of course, and the observer navigated and dropped the bombs. The gunner was also the wireless operator. I found the cockpit configuration took a while to get used to. The pilot sat on the left side of the nose, which was quite cramped, and the flight instruments were in an awkward location. The navigator sat alongside on a sliding seat to perform the bomb aiming. The gunner and wireless operator was situated aft of the wings beside the aircraft's dorsal gun turret.

Getting in and out of a Blenheim was a tight fit when wearing full flying gear, including a jacket, flying boots, and a parachute. We had to climb onto the wing and then maneuver down into the cockpit. Once in the aircraft with engines running, the tips of the propellers were only a foot away from the side windows of the cockpit. Reaching out to give arm signals to ground crews was treacherous, something we often did when flying Fairey Battles.

I soon got to know and feel the Blenheim much better. A few days later, I flew to Dundrum again, south of Belfast, on the Irish Sea, and opposite the Isle of Man. On the way back, I did "air to air" tactics, and to understand the importance of a gunner in a Blenheim, I did a tour in the gun turret. I was air-sick because, unlike fighters, where the guns are fixed, the gunner on a Blenheim is situated in a power-operated turret and can fire from almost any angle to fend off an attacker.

During the first week of June, I flew back and forth between Dundrum and Sydenham many times, doing tactical exercises, towing drogues, and dropping practice bombs. Finally, I had a day off and went into Belfast with some of the crew. On our return, the car got a flat, and we got back at 2 A.M. The next day, on our way up to the mess, we got another flat and spent the morning fixing it. The roads were a bit unpredictable. We were now flying almost every day in good weather and could carry out our scheduled firing and bombing practice. One day, I managed to break off for enough time to swim in the sea. I even got a sunburn.

The war news had not been good recently. The Germans Invaded Greece, and British and Greek forces withdrew to the island of Crete, which was a strategic base in the Eastern Mediterranean. A few of our aircrew had been posted to squadrons in the Mediterranean, and we heard that British forces in North Africa and Egypt were being pushed back from Libya to Tobruk. We continued our routine tactical exercises, air-to-ground, air-to-air, and air-to-sea firing.

On June 22, Churchill spoke over the radio, announcing that Hitler had invaded Russia, ignoring the non-aggression treaty between the two countries, and had given no reason or notice. The Luftwaffe was bombing Russian cities, and German troops were moving east. Churchill also noted that yesterday, the RAF had shot down twenty-eight German aircraft over occupied France. He called on our allies to support Russia. We were aware that if Hitler was able to defeat Russia, Germany would again be able to direct its full force against Britain.

Our squadron had been in Northern Ireland for over six months. There were rumors that we were going to move somewhere, but we had not heard anything official. I wished so much that Bar and I could get away for a few days before our next assignment, so I put in for some leave. It wasn't to be. Our training exercises continued. Sgt. Hardy and I flew to Lisburn, southwest of Belfast, where we were training for low-flying raids on targets on land or water.

It was now the end of June. I had written to my sister. Her birthday was June 30. I was sure my time in Northern Ireland would end soon. I had been in Sydenham with 88 Squadron since last November. We expected our squadron to be moved somewhere, possibly to the Mediterranean or even to Asia. During the past week, the newspapers reported that Blenheim squadrons were bombing Northern France and had pounded Lille and occupied the ports of Brest and La Rochelle. RAF daylight and night-time raids on Cologne, Dusseldorf, Bremen, and the naval base at Kiel had been successful and had been carried out by Blenheims.

The RAF now had stronger control of the air, and our fighter aircraft were able to accompany bombers on their raids. The Luftwaffe was also fighting against Russia on the eastern front. Bomber Command was on the offensive, our squadron had Blenheims, and we were anxious to join the action.

Jean Aylan-Parker (Jimmy's sister) and her son Ronnie with Bar and Michael, at Stutton.

EIGHTEEN

NORFOLK
Summer 1941

Per Ardua ad Astra, the official motto of the RAF, is the Latin for "through adversity to the stars." We all shared a deep commitment to the RAF, our squadron, and our fellow airmen. We wanted to defeat the Germans and were confident we would succeed despite the sacrifices that were being made. At the beginning of July, our squadron was informed that it would be joining No. 2 Group of Bomber Command and moving immediately to the Swanton Morley base in Norfolk. This meant we would see action.

The squadron left Belfast on July 8 for Norfolk. Swanton Morley was a relatively new air base, completed before the war with some long runways for bombers, mostly on grass. The squadrons of No. 2 Group were clustered around the area. Norfolk is on the east coast of England, in the region known as East Anglia, and is closer to the European continent and the targets for RAF bombing raids. When we arrived at Swanton Morley, we were warmly welcomed by the Group Captain and, a few nights later, were given a welcome dinner in the mess with all types of wines and food. It was quite a party, a kind of celebration, and we played "tug of war" and rugby in a mess anti room afterward.

The base was about twenty miles from Norwich, the largest town in Norfolk. We were told that in a few weeks, our squadron would move to a nearby base, probably to Attlebridge, twelve miles outside Norwich. Other squadrons that had been with us in Northern Ireland had moved to bases nearby, and many of the lads I knew would be flying with them. We were all flying Bristol Blenheims.

I had left Ireland without Bar and Michael, who were still in Belfast, and was now faced with a demanding new assignment and the prospect of flying on bombing operations very soon. How would Bar and Michael get over to England and find a place to live near me? Bar had to bring Michael and about fourteen pieces of luggage on what would surely be a challenging journey, given the uncertainties of travel. I was of little help. We decided it was best for her to go to Suffolk and stay at Stutton House until we found a place to live in Norfolk. She had hoped to bring Bridget with her to help care for Michael, but this was not possible because Bridget was from Eire and the British authorities would not let her come over to England. I hoped she might find another person to help her, and the agency in Ireland told us that they would arrange it, but so far, we have not heard anything from them. Without Bridget the journey would be more difficult. When they finally arrived at Stutton, and we talked on the telephone, Bar seemed so happy to be back in England.

She was comfortable staying at Stutton until we could settle somewhere. She had begun to like Ireland, especially as the weather improved and daylight hours were longer, and she had made some good friends there. Knowing that many of them would now be near Norfolk certainly helped, and she said she was looking forward to seeing them again. I wanted so much to get down to Stutton to see her and Michael, but I was very busy settling into the base with my squadron. I thought that on my days off, I might be able to take a bus from Norwich to Ipswich and then down to Stutton, but it would have taken several hours, and there wasn't enough time.

Our base was quite busy. Nothing had the look of permanence. We ate meals in a mess, but the aircrews stayed in billets that were a forty-minute walk away from the hangars, the control tower, the mess hall, and the operations and briefing room. There were various other small buildings and a cinema. A bus ran back and forth from our billets, but you had to know its schedule. A small river nearby had a nice pool where I could take a swim every few days when I had the time. In the evenings, I would try to call Bar on the telephone, but usually, I had to wait a while for a call to get through.

I tried to write letters to her every few days, but I wanted to get down to see her. We had so much to talk about, and I explained that I couldn't say things in my letters to her, so they would have to wait until we were together. One night, I waited so long for my call to her that it still hadn't come through when the last bus to the billets left. I had to walk home.

Our first few days were very busy. We weren't flying yet, but there were many things to prepare. We sometimes had a cricket game after work, and I played for the squadron team, even though I was usually put out on the first ball. I was pretty sure I would see some action soon because the squadrons here and at nearby bases were all part of 2 Group of Bomber Command, and other squadrons were actively carrying out raids over enemy targets. There had been a few changes in our squadron when we left Belfast. One of the Flight Lieutenants was promoted to Squadron Leader, and my friend Dick Shuttleworth was promoted to Flight Lieutenant. Shuttle was being re-assigned to 105 Squadron. We had been together from the beginning: training at Benson, over in France, on the *Lancastria*, and then in Iceland and Northern Ireland. I would miss having him in our squadron. Jack Meakin was promoted to Squadron Leader and posted to another squadron in Norfolk. Jack and I had flown together often. I hoped I would continue to see both Jack and Shuttle. This news was also disappointing for Bar because she and Betty Meakin had been good friends in Ireland, and Bar had hoped to be near her when she moved to Norfolk. There were other chaps who received promotions, but I was left out. I was now the senior flying officer, and I was hoping that I would get a promotion soon. My F/O was dated April 20, 1940. The F/O comes through after serving one year of war service, but my seniority in the RAF is backdated to January 20, 1939, when I signed on.

It was now July 15, and I continued to look for a way to get down to Suffolk to see Bar and Michael. There was no train running from Norwich south to Ipswich, only a bus that would run if there were enough passengers. This didn't sound very reliable. I told Bar that I might try to get a motorbike in Norwich. I tried to call her on the telephone every night, and sometimes I got through. I wrote letters to her almost every day. I knew she felt somewhat alone at Stutton because, unlike an RAF base, there were no young people around for her to meet. Aunt Isabel was very nice, and so was Mrs. Wallace, but the two 'neurotics' could be a bit trying, and Mrs. Wallace was bossed about terribly by Gwen. There were no maids at the house except the cook, so things were a bit hectic.

I kept enquiring and searching for a place for Bar and Michael to live near Norwich. Jack Meakin's Squadron had been posted to Watton, only nine miles from Norwich, and Betty Meakin said she wanted to share a place with Bar somewhere outside of Norwich. She couldn't live close to Jack's base either. We had been told that our squadron was about to move to Attlebridge, only six miles from Norwich, and because of the move, our CO didn't want any of us to be away. It would be another week before anyone would be able to get leave, and I still hadn't seen Bar and Michael since I left Ireland a few weeks ago.

Letters came from home, but not regularly. Some never came. I wrote to my parents and told them that my squadron had moved, but I could not give them any details, of course. I thanked them for sending us the box of food with chocolates and cigarettes and the white knitted sweater and pants for Michael. They all had arrived safely. There were other things we hadn't received that must have gone down at sea. A very special parcel came from Elspeth Laird with jams, sugar, marshmallows, cigarettes, tea, coffee, packs of razor blades, and two flat fifties of Player's mild cigarettes, which Bar and I enjoyed. We were not able to get these things in England. How thoughtful it was of Elspeth to think of us. She is an amazing person and such a good friend of our family. In her letter, she talked about how she was spending the summer at her cottage at Cap-à-l'Aigle on the St. Lawrence River. She said, "I am sitting on the gallery looking at the river and wishing you boys and girls could pop in on your way to Tadoussac like you used to do." She went on, saying, "The CSL 'down' boat is at the Murray Bay wharf, and the 'up' boat should appear round the point at any moment." She had lots of news about people. "The Ted Eberts had a third son and were calling him John. Ted's sister was married to Charlie Price, who was with the Royal Rifles, and while on a few days leave from his regiment, he and Bea went salmon fishing up the Saguenay River."

I felt a little homesick reading all this, but it brought me happy memories of my summers growing up. Elspeth also said that she had her own vegetable garden this summer, as she had done during the last war, except now she was much older. She was getting news of the war and expressed her hope that the Russians would finish off the Germans. She must also have been reading about the RAF and said she hoped that my recent move wasn't to do "those awful raids over the enemy country." According to her, the only sign of war at her place was "we are not allowed any weather reports below Montreal," meaning on St. Lawrence, downriver from Montreal. Presumably, this was to avoid helping the German U-boats that might be there.

By the third week of July, we were hearing more about the operations of other squadrons and their low-flying raids on enemy targets. They were suffering heavy losses of aircraft and crews. Our squadron was still organizing, and although we were flying our

Blenheims, we had yet to engage in operations across the Channel.

Finally, on July 18, I was able to get down to Ipswich to be with Bar and Michael. It was only for 48 hours, but it was so wonderful to be together again. Michael was growing by the day. While I was at Stutton, Gwen showed me her excellent vegetable gardens and a very large bed of onions. I thought the fruit garden was rather disappointing, with only a few peaches, no pears or apples, but a fair number of strawberries and a few gooseberries. Bar quietly told me she had enough of staying at Stutton and really wanted to move. After our forty-eight hours together, I returned to base. We had talked about finding a place to live close to Norwich, but it was difficult for me to look for a place for Bar and Michael because our squadron was expected to move to our new location at the beginning of August, and our C.O. still required us to remain on the base.

Bar asked Jean and Johnny to come up to Stutton for a short visit to be with her, and then she and Michael went down to Borden to be with them. I was able to talk to them both on the phone, and it was so good to hear Jean's voice again. Johnny said he was expecting soon to hear where his unit would be assigned next.

The weather had become warm and a bit hazy, but I was flying on most days now. The new Blenheim IVs had just arrived, and we thought they looked pretty good. We were still flying the old ones, but I expected our flight would be the first to get the new ones. The Blenheim IV was much better armed, faster, and had a longer range. I flew across to Belfast in one of the long-nosed Blenheim IVs and got lost in the mist. It took me three and a half hours to get home.

We practiced low flying frequently, across East Anglia, often at the treetops. It was good training and rather thrilling, and I felt the difference between the Blenheim and the Fairey Battle, especially its agility to fly at very low levels and greater power. After a week of flying the Blenheim IV, I had a better feel for what it could do.

We heard about the other 2 Group squadrons. A recent operation by 105 Squadron had been very successful, and Wing Commander Hughie Edwards had been awarded the VC (Victoria Cross) by His Majesty the King. It was quite an event and very special to have one of your Wing Commanders on the same station awarded a V.C. He was Australian and one of the nicest chaps I have met. He had led twenty Blenheims on a daylight attack at Bremen, which was a highly defended shipbuilding port. On his approach to the German coast over enemy ships, there were no clouds In which to hide. He knew that his raid had been detected and that the enemy defenses would be ready for them.

To reach the target, he led his aircraft 50 miles overland, flying at 50 feet, under and through telephone and high-voltage wires, and through anti-aircraft fire and a balloon barrage. All his aircraft were hit; four were lost, and his own was hit over twenty times, but he brought his remaining aircraft safely home. Earlier in June, Edwards had led six Blenheims in an attack on eight merchant ships in a convoy near The Hague. Flying at a low level, he sunk a 4,000-ton ship. For this, he was awarded the DFC (Distinguished Flying Cross). He was the first in the RAF to be awarded the V.C. and the D.F.C. in this war and the first V.C. I have known. When he was awarded the DFC and asked if he would take it, he said, "No, the only one I want is the victory medal, thanks." They gave it to him just the same. I was sure my father had heard about Edwards and the VC, but I wrote a letter to him about it. I couldn't tell him what was happening now with our bombing operations, so I said, "Life is getting more interesting every day. It's amazing the courage these chaps have got." I think he understood what I meant, but 88 Squadron was still waiting to join the action.

Most evenings at the base, there was something going on. Sometimes, I went to the cinema, but I avoided going into Norfolk with some of the others to drink at the bars. I had given up drinking alcohol to see if it made me feel healthier. One pint of beer a day wouldn't make any difference, but beer was not very cheap these days, so I decided to do without. The mess had some very good ginger beer, so I was drinking that instead. I wished so much that Bar and Michael were closer and we could be together during the evenings. I talked with her on the phone whenever I could get through. It still took about an hour or at least thirty minutes to place a call. She had been feeling lonely, and I knew it must have been difficult for her.

She needed to be with younger people. She asked me how much she should be paying Aunt Isabel while she and Michael were staying at Stutton. I suggested that about two guineas a week should be about right for the two weeks she was there. She was still hoping to get a girl from Ireland to come over to help her. If so, I said that we could find a small furnished house with enough room. The wives of our officers were also looking for places nearby, and many of them were friends she knew from our time in Belfast.

Dick Shuttleworth's fiancé, Honor, who was from Northern Ireland, was staying in Norwich with Dick's family. They had planned their wedding for August 16 in Belfast, and I was hoping to get over there for it. Dick said his car was still in Belfast, but he couldn't get it back here because there wasn't enough petrol available. I thought that if Bar could have a place near Attlebridge, Honor could stay with her. I didn't know when I could go to look for a place, so I thought it might make sense for Bar to come to Norwich and stay in a hotel. In my letters, I told her about our friends from Belfast who were now here with the Squadron. Like us, they were trying to find places to live. Olive Hurnell was still here, and Arthur offered to look for a place for us when he went down to Attlebridge. Arthur Hardy, my observer, and John Briggs, my wireless operator, were looking for a place for their wives near our base. Arthur told me of some large mansion about four or five miles from camp. The owner would let a wing consisting of several rooms, including a dining room and kitchen, but it was said she was very particular. I hadn't heard anything about where the Meakins might have a place. Bar decided that until we had sorted this out, she would stay with Jean and Johnny at their home in Borden. I began to feel that Bar could do much better at looking for a place than I could. She could take a bus to Norwich, but there was an awful lot of luggage to bring for Michael. I so wanted to see her again. I had an empty feeling when I was away from her. The only thing to do was to make the best of it, wherever one was.

The newspapers were full of reports of the war. I read that the Japanese had moved into France's Indo-China colonies and occupied Saigon, provoking the United States to freeze all Japan's assets in America. I wrote a letter to my father because I wondered what this might mean with his new responsibility on Canada's Pacific Coast. He could have his hands full very soon. I said I hoped the US wouldn't want to stop supporting us if they decided to build their defenses in the Pacific. My Parents were living in a place called Esquimalt, outside Victoria, British Columbia. This was the Army base and port for the Royal Canadian Navy on Vancouver Island. The climate there is quite moderate, and undoubtedly, my mother had found a way to do some gardening.

My father's fifty-third birthday was on August 7. I wondered where my parents would live after the War. They might choose Ottawa or Toronto or decide to stay on the west coast, possibly in Victoria. How different this war would seem to my father after the one he fought two decades ago. It was certainly not pleasant, but then, war was not intended to be. It is not only soldiers, sailors, and airmen who are in it; the people are, too. Bar had already seen a good share of what it was like. In this war, the Air Force has a key role, and just the other day, I read an article from the *Sunday People* in London that said that "the RAF offensive is the vital part of our war plan. It is the new strategy." I also wrote a letter to my cousin Nan for her birthday and to my Uncle Jack and Aunt Mary Wallace, thanking them for the three packs of Sweet Caporal cigarettes they sent over.

It was the last week of July when our squadron began flying actual bombing operations, our targets being coastal shipping and enemy-occupied ports on the Channel. It is amazing how different one feels on the real thing. I thought of my hockey and how playing the actual game felt so different from our practices. However, on a bombing raid, we flew with the full knowledge that some of us might not return. We lived with the hope that it wouldn't be us.

Bar and Michael were still staying with Jean and Johnny, and it was fortunate that they were able to help. She also kept in touch with Mary and Ted. I asked her to give my best to Jean and Johnny and a hug for my nephew, Ronnie. I tried to talk to her every evening on the telephone, and I would tell her whether I had flown that day. We were often up at 4:30 for take-off at 6, depending on the weather, and back by noon. Bar knew that I was flying on raids over enemy targets. She didn't know the details of our raids, and anyhow, I wasn't allowed to tell her, but she was aware that some of our crews were missing or had been lost in action. She certainly knew that No. 2 Group's squadrons were carrying out raids over enemy targets and were experiencing losses. She was very brave, and I think it helped that she was always busy. Our letters and our conversations on the phone at night were all we had, and it was disappointing when the calls didn't get through.

It was July 28, and everything was ready for us to move to our squadron's new base. The days were getting shorter and darker earlier. Art Hurnell and I had no lights in the room we were sharing. Weather was always a major factor in the decision to fly. Several times, our flight was ready to go when our operations were called off at the last minute because of the weather. Forecasting weather was difficult, especially when we would be returning home from the target. Electric storms could affect our instruments and could make the compass unusable. Navigators frequently used features we recognized on the ground to follow our course, and on a clear night, they sometimes used the stars.

Wind speed could vary, and it was difficult to measure. It could cause the aircraft to go off course or run short of petrol. Each day at 2 Group Bomber Command, the decisions on operations depended on the meteorologists. Good weather for bombing wasn't always good weather for flying, and when you returned from a raid, you could face the worst: fog over the airdrome, fuel was low, the crew was tired, and the aircraft had been damaged. You landed at a higher risk.

Our training had included extensive low flying in our Blenheims. We flew low over the sea to avoid detection by the enemy. We would shoot up over landfall, still flying low over fields toward our target. One day, I landed back at the base with some laundry attached to my tail wheel. It was not uncommon for Blenheims to return home trailing different kinds of vegetation. The speed of the plane, the dust kicking up off the ground, and the need to get out of there and up for cloud protection made flying quite challenging. Training and experience were so important because everything we did had elements of danger. A couple of days before, one of our chaps was killed in a collision on the airdrome.

At the end of July, I received the good news that my promotion to Flight Lieutenant came through. I was really pleased. Many of my pals had left 88 Squadron and been posted elsewhere. Dick Shuttleworth had been made Squadron Leader in 105 Squadron. Jack Roe, a great pal of mine, had been posted out to the Far East. Jack Meakin was promoted to Squadron Leader and posted to another squadron nearby. Another of my friends who was posted to Malta had just sunk an eight-thousand-ton ship in the Mediterranean.

I was pleased that they were becoming senior officers, but I felt frustrated that I wasn't moving ahead faster. In a letter to my parents, I said, "Sometimes I feel that I don't seem to be doing anything more spectacular than being an unofficial test pilot." Of course, all these ranks are "acting," but with pay. I was still in the early stages of my operations tour, which was likely to be around thirty "ops'. I would have lots of chances to prove myself.

On August 1, our squadron moved to Attelbridge, and we received 19 Blenheim MK IVs. I was enjoying my flying very much now, and it was certainly more challenging. All squadrons of 2 Group were on bombing raids almost daily in good weather and sometimes at night. Our targets continued to be factories located in the German-occupied countries of France, Belgium, and Holland, as well as Germany itself. There was a concentration on coastal shipping near the occupied ports along the enemy coasts. Frequent targets were Calais, Boulogne, and Brest, where German capital ships and a U-boat base were located. We never knew what our targets would be until the morning of the raid. On the days we were flying, we had the traditional English breakfast of bacon and eggs, followed by our briefing, where our commanding officer described the day's operations.

We sat on rows of benches in the briefing room, facing curtains behind which was a large map of the Continent. Everything on the base was now top security, no calls out or in. When the curtains in the briefing room were drawn closed, our route was displayed on the map with a tape to show our course across the Channel and the turn we would make towards our target. The importance of our operation was explained along with the expected weather, enemy ground defenses, and the probability of meeting Luftwaffe fighters. After the CO wished us "good luck," we waited around the crew room until it was time. When called, we suited up, removing anything personal from our pockets in case we were captured. We collected our parachutes and Mae West life vests and climbed into the vans that took us out to our aircraft. This was always hard on the nerves and much worse than the butterflies I used to have before playing hockey at college. We understood the reality of what we were being asked to do. I thought about how I got here, the training I had received, and I was well prepared. The war had to be fought, and I would do my part.

Our fighter squadrons were now flying with us on our raids, and Fighter Squadron 152 had arrived at Swanton Morley with Supermarine Spitfire Mk IIAs. They could give us protection to the Dutch coast or as far as their flying range would allow. On our raids on enemy shipping between Brittany and the coast of Norway, we would fly across the Channel or the North Sea, often at wave-top height to avoid detection. Enemy ships usually sailed close to shore, and there was always the chance they had destroyer escorts or the Luftwaffe, yet being near shore also gave us the chance to turn inland to attack enemy troops or equipment near the coast. Flying low at high speed just above the ground can be exciting.

On August 12, squadrons from 2 Group carried out a major raid on two large German power stations near Cologne. Jack Meakin was the squadron leader for one of the formations, and when he told me about it afterward, I wished so much that 88 Squadron and my flight had been part of it. There were 54 Blenheims involved on a daylight operation, which included six flights from Jack's Squadron 82. It was the biggest and most ambitious operation ever undertaken by the RAF, and it turned out to be a great success.

The Blenheims were escorted by our Spitfires and Hurricanes as far as the Belgian border. According to Jack, they flew low over the sea, and as they crossed the Dutch farmlands at tree-top height, people on the ground waved at them and cheered them on. They crossed into Germany to their target, the largest steam power plant in Europe called Knapsack, just west of Cologne. Jack led his flights on a low-flying approach, and they were met with intense flak. After dropping delayed action bombs on the target, they were able to see the damage done as they turned for home but were soon attacked by Me 109 "snappers."

Of the 54 Blenheims on this raid, twelve were lost. Jack was awarded the DFC (Distinguished Flying Cross) for his leadership. Hearing about a successful operation like this was encouraging, and I felt very good for him.

All our operations required crossing water, and the return could be very difficult because of weather changes or damage to our aircraft. We were trained for what to do if we had to ditch. When the aircraft hit the water, it would pull up suddenly, and we had to signal our position immediately. We were already wearing Mae Wests, the dinghy was provisioned with rations, and we were told to exercise to stay warm. On our return from raids, it was not unusual for an aircraft to ditch, especially if damaged. We had to fly low over water for miles in both directions and in all kinds of unpredictable weather. Low-level flying over water demands a pilot's full concentration, and misty conditions can make it difficult to judge your height. The prospect of ditching on the sea was very real.

A very successful raid was carried out on August 16 by 2 Group squadrons, this time on Rotterdam, one of the largest occupied ports where the Germans were using the factories and warehouses to supply their coastal shipping. Our squadron was not part of this attack, but we heard that our Blenheims flew very low across the fields to remain undetected and to surprise enemy ships near the harbor. Forty-thousand tons of shipping were destroyed. Each aircraft, flying low over the docks, could pick out and go after its target, a ship, factory, or equipment. There had been only light anti-aircraft fire, and German fighters were absent and may have been drawn elsewhere.

While most of us loved flying bombers, it was physically and mentally demanding. As a pilot, I always felt the stress on take-off and landing, and flying a bomber for several hours required continuous concentration. Aircrews operate under considerable strain. Hardy and Briggs were very capable. We worked together as a team, each knowing and doing our part: flying, navigation, gunnery, and bombing. There is a rigid discipline, and every detail must be checked. We flew together for hours in cramped space and freezing temperatures, sometimes nineteen below zero, wearing layers of clothing, and sometimes we used oxygen. We depended on each other in our efforts to find the target, avoid enemy defenses, and deal with weather and, if they happened, mechanical problems and injuries. As pilot, I had full responsibility for my crew, and we were committed to each other and to the other crews who flew with us.

As aircrew on a Blenheim, we were only borrowing our aircraft to fly. Our ground crew was very important, and we knew that the aircraft really belonged to them. They maintained it, made sure that everything functioned correctly, and repaired any damage we or the enemy might have done to it during our raids. At take-off, they helped us climb aboard and start up our engines, and they wished us well as we taxied for take-off. When we returned and landed, the "Erks," as they were fondly called, greeted us, thankful that we and the aircraft were safe. We went on our way, but their work had just begun.

Our bombing operations increased, and all No. 2 Group's Blenheim squadrons were now actively engaged. On most raids, several squadrons took part. The RAF had been successful at destroying the enemy's railways, and this might have forced them to use coastal shipping to move their supplies from one place to another. There were reports that the occupied ports were busier than ever with traffic. It was obvious to all of us that Bomber Command was mounting a deliberate offensive with more frequent raids.

However, the enemy coasts were very well defended, and we were losing aircraft and crews almost daily on the low-flying daylight raids. Our officers in senior ranks participated as members of our aircrews because of their experience. They were not invulnerable, and recently, 2 Group had lost six Wing Commanders in one week. This had to be a reason for the frequent promotions. I had flown at one time or another with many of the others in my squadron, and the bonds we felt grew stronger the more we flew together. I cared deeply about what happened to them.

The high casualty rates were a strain on everyone, especially when the lads we knew didn't return. Sometimes, I found myself thinking that I really might not make it through the war. On most of the raids, we usually lost one aircraft, but often, we lost more. They were reported as "missing," and we hoped they landed safely, even if they had been captured, but we knew that some were gone. One can become immune to the daily reports of casualties, but not when they are lads you know and have just been flying with.

The pressure on us continued daily, and we had little time to rest. Our cricket games were less frequent. I tried to avoid letting it get to me. I prayed for those who flew with me and those who didn't return. This helped, and my faith reminded me that God intends a life for each of us, and we should live it knowing he cares for us. When I remembered the motto of RMC: "Truth, Duty, Valour," it gave me comfort and helped me to endure the pressure and to carry on.

My worries might have been obvious to my parents from a letter I had written. I asked them about the two life insurance policies I had left in Canada in case my ship had been sunk on my way over to England. One for $1,000 was with the Manufacturer's Life, the other for $3,000 with the Edinburgh Standard Life Assurance. Neither had coverage for inflight loss, and the Scottish one did not have war coverage but would have had a cash value. I also did not have a will, which meant that if I was killed, everything of mine would be Bar's. Because letters from Canada often took a month to reach us, and some never came at all, we decided to number each of our letters to know which ones never arrived.

It was early August when I told Bar about my promotion. She decided to come up to Norwich and leave Michael with Jean so she could look for a place for them to live. She agreed that she might do better than I had at finding a place. "The bus will take you directly from the station up to the Bell Hotel on the Castle," I wrote. "Norwich is quite a good place for shops, so it shouldn't be too bad up here. When you get here, don't be afraid to spend money on taxis or anything like that because you don't want to waste time on trying to get about looking for a place." And I added. 'I miss you so much, and I always have an empty feeling somewhere inside me when I am away from you. We have to keep making the best of it."

Bar arrived and found a delightful little home called "Rose Cottage." She was very pleased with it, and Betty Meakin said she would live with her because Jack's squadron was at another base nearby. Bar stayed for a few days at the Bell Hotel in the center of town. It is an historic coaching inn built in 1485, and the food was very good, especially the seafood from the coast, probably from Yarmouth. Unfortunately, seafood didn't agree with Bar, but she enjoyed the freshwater fish. She had to return to Jean's in Borden to bring Michael to Stutton and collect their things there before moving up to Norwich. On the train to Stutton, Bar said that Michael sat up and talked to everyone; not bad considering all he could say was "DaDa" and "Mamam" and other noises if you could figure them out. I wrote to my parents, saying, "Jean thought he would be a scholar and seems to have a great liking for printed matter rather than any toys."

I thought of my parents often, and at times, I missed them terribly. They seemed so far away. I wrote regularly, and recently, I referred to my father's responsibilities and said, "I expect you are watching Japan pretty keenly these days and how it might affect the British Columbia coast." I told them that the Cowichan Siwash sweater they sent hadn't arrived and must have gone down and that my Uncle Sydney had arrived in England and had written to me that before he left Canada, he had been in Tadoussac, and it seemed very empty with only four people in our family house.

It is interesting what you think about when you are so far away from those you love. I couldn't remember whether my brother Ronnie's birthday was in July or August, and I was embarrassed to have to ask my parents. I realized it was August 27, and I wanted to send him a present, but many things were not allowed to be sent out of the country, so I wrote him a letter and asked him about his pet rabbits.

Bar and Michael settled into "Rose Cottage" on August 12. It was ideally situated on the bus line and next door to a pub. It also had a telephone. It was close enough that I was able to get over in the evenings quite frequently, and when I had a day off, I could stay overnight. I never told Bar when I was going on a raid, but on my return, I would try to fly over the house so she would know I was back. I told her, "I flew over Stutton the other day, only a few feet above the trees, so I expect Aunt Isabel heard me all right. Strangely enough, I was doing an exercise, and I wasn't just shooting up."

Dick Shuttleworth and Honor were married in Belfast, and all his friends in the squadron sent a poetic telegram wishing them well. However, because of the intensity of our bombing operations, Dick was called back to his squadron immediately, and their honeymoon was interrupted, but he was able to get permission to stay with Honor at the local pub in Norwich. The Commander of Bomber Command Group No. 2 believed in aggressive attacks with low-flying daylight raids.

Our casualties were very high, and we were losing chaps almost daily. I had just heard that Jack Roe had been killed. His squadron had been sent to Malta on the Mediterranean. He was a peach of a fellow and had been one of my best friends in Northern Ireland. We cannot control our fate. You have a rough sense of the odds of being hit or crashing, but you go on hoping that it won't happen to you.

I wondered if Bar had noticed the stress that I had been under during the past few weeks. I tried to hide it. She hadn't said anything, but one night, I woke up around two in the morning and found her awake. She told me she hadn't been able to get to sleep. I had been so preoccupied with my flying that I hadn't thought about what she was going through. She had put up with a lot during the fifteen months we had been married. Our times together were wonderful and happy, but we had been apart when I was in Iceland and Northern Ireland. Now, at last, we were together, just as I had become heavily engaged in offensive operations. I began to appreciate the courage Bar needed to live with all this. Spending time with her was comforting, and we were very happy together. During the evenings, we talked about the past and dreamed of what our future might be like after the war. We wondered where we would live. My career with the RAF might move us to other places in the world. Where would Michael grow up and go to school?

Would we be able to spend summers in Tadoussac with our family? We both wanted Michael to enjoy it as we had. What would the world be like when this war was over? Sometimes, we simply relaxed by reading to each other. My anxiety about our flying must have begun to show, and one evening, I told her that I didn't expect to survive through all the raids we were being ordered to fly. "You mustn't say that," she said. Bar always looked at the happy side of life and the way to enjoy it.

The heavy demands on our squadrons continued, and our operations were now directed at enemy coastal shipping. Attacking ships and convoys was challenging because they were frequently protected by flak ships and destroyers, and Luftwaffe fighters could suddenly arrive to pick off our Blenheims. To attack a convoy, we had to fly very low, partly for surprise but also because Me 109s would try to get below us where we were most vulnerable until we could get up into the clouds. A Blenheim is quite maneuverable, but it took skill to fly so low on a bombing attack, avoid flak, and get away into the clouds.

On August 26, I flew on one of these operations to the North Sea and Heligoland, about forty miles off the coast of Germany near Bremen and Hamburg. 88 Squadron had nine Blenheims organized into three flights: A, B, and C. We were led by our CO, a Wing Commander, and each flight of three aircraft was led by a squadron leader. After our briefing at 800 hrs., we collected our parachutes and Mae Wests, suited up, and rode out to our aircraft. We checked over everything before starting engines and took off on a slow climb out over the Channel toward the North Sea, flying low at around 100 feet above the water. We flew in formation, and at times, we were protected by cloud cover. It was left to us to attack a ship when we saw one. In my flight with me was Alan Lynn, our squadron leader, and we spotted a convoy in the distance. Flying low, we were on it very soon, and I picked out a ship. I made the attack, flying the Blenheim about twenty feet above the water to avoid the ship's anti-aircraft guns. I came in at the height of its masts and then lifted high enough to drop our bombs and get out of there. It was tricky because I had to clear the ship and avoid banking that would expose our belly to the ship's anti-aircraft fire. This required a skidding turn while making sure our wingtip missed hitting the water. We managed to score a direct hit on the ship, and she sank. My crew was jubilant. We had sunk a four-thousand-ton ship. We lost one aircraft from our flight, but I must admit that it was hard not to feel good about what we accomplished. I also felt very pleased with the Blenheim's maneuverability, flying at low levels. We headed for home and were fortunate not to meet any Luftwaffe fighters.

The next day, I was off duty and able to spend the whole day with Bar and some time with Michael, who was enjoying his large English pram. That evening, I invited my crew, John Briggs and Arthur Hardy, to come over to Rose Cottage for dinner with us. We had a fun time, and Michael was intent on being part of it as they were all very interested in him. John and Arthur were very capable air sergeants, and we had been flying together as a team for what now seemed like an age. Each of them entertained us with stories about growing up with their families, and we had lots of laughs. They left early, and I had a few minutes alone with Bar before returning to the base. I was pretty certain we would be flying again in the morning, but I didn't say anything to her about it. I didn't want to add to her worry. I hated to leave. I knew the next day would be busy for me, and it would go by quickly. But for Bar, it would be different. She would be waiting, not knowing. She'd be wondering when I would return to base. She wouldn't rest until she heard my plane fly over Rose Cottage. Then she'd know I was home.

Bristol Blenheims flying in formation.

AUGUST 28, 1941, 17:39
Attlebridge Airfield, Norfolk, England

It's been a long day, and we're still here. But the weather has finally cleared, and we just got our orders to go. The vans take us pilots out to our aircraft. The ground crews have everything ready. Arthur Hardy, my Observer, is the first to climb on board. He takes his spot in the gunner turret. I climb into the cockpit, while John Briggs, my Navigator, takes his place beside me. We go through the checks. Once done, I signal to the ground crew that we are all set. Then, we are given clearance to go.

As soon as I start the engines, I feel the aircraft come to life. The tension I've been holding all day suddenly evaporates as I focus on the task at hand. It's now impossible to hear each other talk without the use of headphones.

The ground crew has removed the chocks holding our wheels. I release the brakes and open the throttle. We are on the move, taxiing into formation behind our squadron leader, Alan Lynn. I know what I have to do now. This is what I've trained for. I am ready.

As we take off, climbing up into the late afternoon sky with our load of bombs, I look out over the bright green of the English countryside beneath us. The setting sun is behind us as we head east northeast towards Coltishall and then out over the North Sea. We are on course at last, flying low towards our target, the Port of Rotterdam.

Bombing of the port of Rotterdam, August 28, 1941.

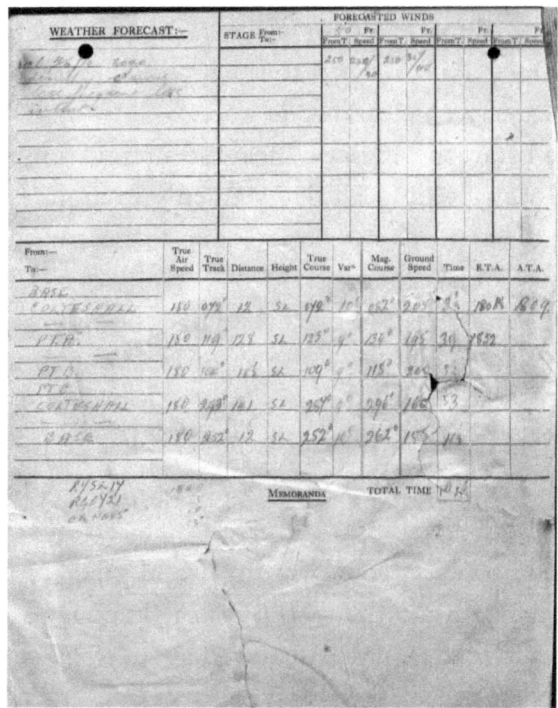

Flight record retrieved from the wreckage of Jimmy's plane.

AFTERWORD

88 Squadron's Blenheims returned to base later that evening. Bar heard their engines in the distance and waited, but Jimmy didn't fly over Rose Cottage that night. Earlier that day, about the time she imagined he might be over the target, she had a premonition. She had a strange feeling, as if he was in the room with her, and then he was gone. She feared the worst and decided to call the base to find out what happened. After several rings, a male voice answered. She could hear noise in the background of the aircrews gathering in the mess. She asked about Jimmy. The voice hesitated and gave her an inconclusive response. Bar knew. What she had felt during the raid was real.

She was alone with Michael – and so thankful she had him. She called her sister Mary, and Ted arrived almost immediately. "He poured me a scotch," she said. "I never drank scotch, before or since, but it really helped." Soon, letters arrived from home comforting and expressing hope that Jimmy was alive. His father knew the odds and wrote: "If that dear gallant life had to end, thank God it ended suddenly and was not prolonged by perhaps years of suffering as is the case with many of his contemporaries."

It is customary that a Commanding Officer communicate with the wives of crews missing on raids. Jimmy's squadron leader, an Australian who he had described as a good friend, talked with Bar. He had been on the Rotterdam raid with Jimmy and told her that during the raid, there was so much happening that it was difficult to know how Jimmy was shot down. The RAF reported Jimmy and his crew as "missing in action." There had been no confirmation that they had been killed.

Bar wrote to Jimmy's parents.

> *"I know that just after seven that evening, something happened, and that was when they were over the target. Jimmy wouldn't want us to be unhappy. He hated to see anyone unhappy, and he was always happy himself. He is safe and happy now. If he has gone, or if a prisoner which, please God, he is, he is seeing another part of the world, which he wouldn't otherwise be seeing, and he always wanted to see new places."*

In October, Bar received notice through the Red Cross that official German information had confirmed that Jimmy had been killed immediately. A year later, when describing that day, she said that she knew Jimmy had been killed, even though he was reported as "missing in action."

About the Rotterdam Raid on August 28, 1941

Aircraft reconnaissance and photographs indicated that the Germans were using the docks and the Port of Rotterdam to assemble war materials and a large fleet of merchant ships to supply key locations along the coast of occupied countries on the continent. An August 16th raid on Rotterdam proved very successful. There was moderate anti-aircraft fire from the ground and no sign of defense from German fighters. Jimmy had not been part of that raid. The August 28 raid on Rotterdam was a very different story.

In the book *Bomber's Battle*, a Wing Commander describes what happened:

> *On August 28, a force of Blenheims from Squadrons 21, 88, and 110 set off, this time with an escort of Spitfire fighters. As soon as they reached the mouth of the Nieuwe Waterweg, the canal which links Rotterdam to the sea, destroyers and the land offenses put up a heavy barrage. The enemy was not to be surprised again. Their fighters were already on patrol, and as the Blenheims came through the barrage, the Me 109s were ready for them.*
>
> *The Blenheims went in over the docks at between 20 and 50 feet; they were met by a hail of light anti-aircraft shells and machine gun bullets. In spite of many hits on German installations, too many British aircraft were lost. The Germans destroyed seven Blenheims and at least two Spitfires. The end of one of them had been seen by other crews. Crossing low over the docks through heavy gunfire, it crashed into a warehouse, which immediately took fire.*

The London Sunday Times also reported on the raid:

> *Flying at between 20ft and 50ft, our Blenheims scooped down on the docks at Rotterdam on Thursday afternoon. The attack was delivered in line abreast. Two made for a large ship at the southwest end of Maashaven. The first got a hit on the stern, and when the second had bombed, its crew saw the ship entirely obscured by bursts. Another Blenheim hit a large ship amidships. A fire broke out, and the smoke which poured up was reddened with flames. Many other ships were attacked, both in the docks and in the slipways where they were building. Columns of smoke rose from the shipyards,*

and bombs burst among cranes, wharf machinery, and sheds on the quayside. A warehouse burst into flames, and the fire quickly spread. Some of the Blenheims were hit even before they reached the docks, but they continued through the anti-aircraft fire and sent their bombs down. Aircraft which have not returned were seen to make successful attacks.

The Vrij Nederland, the free Dutch newspaper published in London, made this report:

A Dutchman who was in Rotterdam when the RAF Blenheims made their recent devastating raid on shipping and the docks tells an amazing story: "The audacious raid was a terrific success," he said. "Not only was great damage done in one of the main shipbuilding yards, but a great number of ships were sunk including one German destroyer. It was like an aerobatic display because the British planes came skimming over the town. One of them came down in the very center of Rotterdam."

The tactics for the August 28 Rotterdam raid were a repetition of the earlier raid that was highly successful. It was pointed out by one squadron leader that "this time, the Germans would be ready for us."

According to Martin Bowman in his book *Daylight Bombing Operations 1939-1942*, when the Blenheims took off, there was considerable anxiety about the outcome. He wrote:

The first attempt, just after 14:40, was recalled at 15:30. At 17:20, 18 crews on 21, 88, 110, and 226 Squadrons were off successfully, though 'F-Freddie' on 226 Squadron crashed on take-off. Spitfires IIs on 19 Squadron and 152 Squadron provided fighter escort and were picked up, and the formation flew to a point four miles south of Oostvoorm, where they would turn to their second point five miles south of Waalhaven where the three boxes of aircraft would come into line abreast and speed in at roof-top height.

The formation made landfall at the Dutch coast, but when they reached the mouth of the Nieuwe Waterweg, the canal that links Rotterdam to the sea, destroyers and anti-aircraft batteries threw up a terrific barrage of flack. As soon as they were clear of the flack, they came under attack from enemy fighters. One Messerschmitt 109F pierced the screen of Spitfires to engage a Blenheim but was immediately chased away. The Blenheims flew on, hugging the ground all the way to the docks.

Their arrival was greeted with a hail of light machine gun and flack fire as they swept across Rotterdam at roof-top height in line abreast. The Spitfires, meanwhile, had climbed to 1,500 feet to provide top cover while the Blenheims went in over the docks at between twenty and fifty feet and hurled their bombs into shipping and construction yards. They were met by a hail of light anti-aircraft shells and machine gun bullets – there was even rifle fire from the ground.

The attack was successful in causing lots of damage, but it was not made without losses.

The official report of Jimmy's aircraft:

August 28, 1941
Blenheim IV Z 7445 No. 88 Squadron, Swanton Morley
Flight Lieutenant James Okeden Alexander
Observer: Flight Sergeant Alexander James Hardy
Wireless Operator/Air Gunner: Flight Sergeant John Lionel Briggs

Their plane was hit and went down on a slaughterhouse in Schiedam in the port of Rotterdam. Schiedam is located on the waterway into the harbor from the Hook of Holland. The log prepared by John Briggs was later retrieved from the wreckage and shows the aircraft as having left the base at Attlebridge on a course of 82º, at a ground speed of 205 mph. It is clear from the log that they passed over the town of Coltishall at 18:09. From there they would have turned southeast to cross the Channel towards Rotterdam. Their ETA for their first target (PT. A) was logged for 18:52. But there was no ATA. It is believed that they were shot down sometime before 19:00. A photograph was taken of Z7445 after it crashed and is retained at Nederlands Instituut voor Militaire Historie.

Another Blenheim lost that day, along with four Blenheims from 21 Squadron, was flown by Jimmy's good friend, Dick Shuttleworth.

Things Go Wrong in War

On August 29, the day following the raid, Winston Churchill gave this tribute to the RAF crews:

> *The devotion of the attacks on Rotterdam are beyond all praise. The charge of the Light Brigade at Balaclava is eclipsed in brightness by these daily deeds of fame.*

Privately, he wrote to his chief of air staff saying:

> *The loss of seven Blenheims out of seventeen in the daylight attack on merchant shipping and docks at Rotterdam is most severe. While I greatly admire the bravery of the pilots, I do not want them pressed too hard. Easier targets giving a high damage return compared to casualties may be more often selected.*

Afterword 229

Wreckage of Jimmy's plane. Bristol Blenheim IV, Wing Number Z7445, hull code RH-M of the 88 Squadron of the RAF at the slaughterhouse in Schiedam.

During the month of August, the rate of loss was around 30%. Of the seventy-seven Blenheims that attacked shipping, twenty-three were lost.

Questions were later raised as to whether the risks taken were necessary given the probability of such great losses.

In his book *Bomber Command*, Max Hastings refers to the slaughter of 2 Group's Blenheims on anti-shipping operations and their Commanding Officer, Air Vice Marshall Donald Stevenson:

> *Many wartime bomber command officers attracted controversy, but few such universal dislike as Stevenson. He was christened "Butcher," not with the rueful affection with which the name was later attached to (Air Marshall) Harris, but with bitter resentment. An arrogant, ruthless man with no apparent interest in the practical problems facing his crews, Stevenson seemed to regard 2 Group's operations solely in the light of their value to his own advancement. "A ship hit is a ship sunk!" he declared emphatically as he compiled willfully*

and grossly exaggerated statistics of his Group's achievements. Losses did not disconcert him at all.

Max Hastings observed that:

Much has been said and written about Fighter Command in 1940. Yet the sacrifice of Bomber Command's 2 Group was also the stuff of which legends are made. It was their tragedy that few of them were left to tell of it. During 1941, RAF aircraft losses grew alarmingly. During the first 18 nights of August 1941, 107 aircraft were lost. The entire front line of Bomber command had been statistically wiped out in less than four months.

In December 1941, Air Vice Marshall Donald Stevenson, the AOC of 2 Group Bomber Command, was removed from his command.

Sir Arthur Harris, Marshal of the RAF and Bomber Command, wrote this:

Remember that these crews, shining youth on the threshold of life, lived under circumstances of intolerable strain. They were, in fact – and they knew it – faced with the virtual certainty of death, probably in one of its least pleasant forms. They knew, well enough, that they owed their circumstances to the stupidity, negligence, and selfishness of the older generations who, since 1918, had done little to avert another war and even less to prepare for it.

The RAF losses in August 1941 continued in September and October. In a period of about four months, Bomber Command lost a major part of its experienced aircrews. According to Charles Patterson, in his book *Daylight Bombing*, "The casualty rate on

Blenheims in 2 Group was such that statistically you could not survive more than 7 to 10 Operations, but you had to do 30."

During World War II, 51% of RAF Bomber Command's aircrews were killed in operations, 12% were killed or wounded in non-operational accidents, and 13% became Prisoners of war. Only 27% survived unscathed. When compared with World War I, these airmen had less chance of survival than those who fought in the trenches. More of them were killed than in the London Blitz or the bombing of Hamburg or Dresden.

Bar Returns to Canada, November 1941

Bar remained in England for several months, hoping that she might hear some news about Jimmy. In October, when the RAF informed her that through the Red Cross, German authorities confirmed that he had been killed, she realized that without Jimmy, a life in England was now in question. She loved England, and although her sister and sister-in-law were there, she knew they would return to Canada when the war was over. Canada was home for her and for most of Jimmy's family. Who knew what England or Canada would be like when the war was over? Her childhood friends were in Canada. She knew that Jimmy's family would embrace her as one of them. She and Michael sailed from Liverpool on the M.V. *Langibby Castle* (Union Castle Line) and landed in Halifax, Nova Scotia, on November 24, 1941, two weeks before the United States entered the war.

Bar returned to her parent's home in Montreal. She and Michael lived on the third floor of their house on McGregor Street, until the war ended in 1945. When her father died, the house was sold, and she and Michael moved to a small apartment over a garage on Wood Avenue in Westmount. In April of 1948, she married Captain Alistair Campbell, who had returned from the war after serving with the Canadian Artillery in Italy. She and Alistair had three daughters, Catherine, Barbara and Jill.

What Others Said About Jimmy

When telling her grandchildren about the war and her experiences in England, Bar said:

> *"No one will ever know what those years when we were young meant to us, and I can look back knowing that I was so lucky to have had them and also know that my children, grandchildren, and great-grandchildren can be proud of the example left to them by Jimmy's life, short though it was."*

Crawford Grier, the headmaster of BCS when Jimmy was at the school, had a great fondness for him. He had seen the letter Jimmy wrote to his parents on the sinking of the *Lancastria* describing his experience – the lengthy evacuation, the bombing, and thousands in the water seeking rescue. He highlighted the letter in the *BCS Magazine* yearbook and celebrated Jimmy's award of the life-saving medal from the Royal Humane Society. In his letter to Bar after Jimmy was killed, he offered a free education for Michael at BCS.

In his memoirs, Jimmy's father, Ronald Alexander, described Jimmy's graduation from Bishop's College School. Jimmy was already enrolled at RMC when he returned to BCS for the prize-giving in September 1935:

> *"His grandfather, who was still Bishop of Quebec, gave away the prizes. Jimmy had done extremely well during the last three years of his school career, but this was his crowning day. In his RMC uniform, looking very self-conscious but with his sweet, shy smile, he went up time and time again to receive many prizes at the hands of his grandfather. It was the proudest day of my life. Jimmy's school career had been brilliant. In addition to his academic prizes and finishing as a Head Boy, he played on the 1st hockey, cricket, and*

rugby football teams. He won the tennis cup, a gold medal for shooting, the intermediate gym competition, and was a Sergeant in the Cadet Corps."

His Mother, Gertrude, wrote in 1941:

"His sister Jean always adored him. I remember how terribly hurt she was when he first began to prefer other peoples' sisters to his own. It's so true about Jim always being happy. I think his life has been an absolutely happy one. He hated to see others unhappy, and he hated to hear anyone criticized. He was very tolerant of his fellow men and hated to hear anyone talking like gossip."

In a letter to a friend, she wrote:

"We can only hope that this great sacrifice of so many of the gallant youth may be for a final peace, but then it's awful to think of so much sorrow to come too. I find it hard to believe that anyone as joyous and full of life as our son Jim can be no more. Perhaps one can still pray for a miracle and hope secretly in one's heart that it might be so."

A BCS old boy, John Churchill Smith, wrote. "Jimmy Alexander was a man who should not be killed. He would have had a leading position in this country (Canada) after the War."

The RMC class of 1939 was a close bunch. Most went on to careers in the military, and over half of them had immediate officer commissions. World War II began three months after their graduation, and many of the class lost their lives. Each of them had that silver gong on which the names of their classmates were inscribed. Those who survived the war continued their friendships. Some, including Jimmy, Ted Price, Ken Ward, Hugh Morrisey,

Chou Price, and John Stairs, had children who grew up knowing each other. Jimmy's great friend and classmate Michael MacBrien, who joined the RCAF, was killed when his aircraft crashed in January 1941. He is buried in Beechwood Cemetery in Ottawa.

In 1941, Jimmy was 23; Bar was 22

Years Later

Betty Lynn wrote to Bar in 1946. Jimmy and Bar had known her and her husband Alan in Belfast and Norfolk with the Squadrons.

In 1981, Bar received a Christmas card from Dick Shuttleworth's widow, Honor. Dick was also killed during the August 28, 1941 Rotterdam raid. Honor remarried (McConnell) and returned home to Northern Ireland to live in Holywood, County Down.

Bar's friend Elisabeth, her classmate in school at Marlow, Bucks, U.K, returned to Norway before the war and they lost touch. When the war was over, they reconnected and wrote letters to each other for years. Bar went to Oslo with Michael to see Elisabeth long after the War and they had a happy reunion.

Jimmy's grave in Crooswijk Cemetary, Rotterdam, 1941.

The Cemetery in Rotterdam

In 1959, Bar made her first visit after the war to Jimmy's grave at Crooswijck Cemetery in Rotterdam. She brought Michael with her. It is a beautiful civilian cemetery with a section at the back where one hundred and twenty-four airmen killed on the Allies' raids on German-occupied ports and factories in Holland are buried. Most were under the age of twenty-five. They are British, Canadian, Australian, New Zealand, and some Americans. The Dutch buried them here secretly against strict prohibition by the German occupiers. Shortly after Jimmy was buried, a photograph of the white wooden cross on his grave was sent by underground and reached his grandparents. The letter from the person who took the photo says:

> *This photo was taken by me when it was absolutely forbidden by the Germans to take any photos at all. I ask you kindly to send this photo to one of the families of those who died together with my deep respects from Rotterdam, Holland.*
>
> *In Holland, we are very grateful for the sacrifices made by these men, and we sincerely hope God will help those left behind to bear their losses.*
> *With deep sympathy,*
> *I.H. Colewy*
> *Blockandstraat 48*
> *Rotterdam*

The wooden crosses have long since been replaced by stone memorials showing the name, service, rank, date of death, and other affiliations.

Bar made numerous visits to the cemetery in Rotterdam, always carrying a basket of flowers, which she placed in front of Jimmy's grave. Jimmy's grandchildren and some of his great-grandchildren have visited his grave.

Her last visit in 2005 at age 86 was on a warm and sunny day. She carried flowers and wore her RAF "Wings" brooch. Placing the flowers before Jimmy's grave, she knelt, and with her left hand, she began digging the ground behind the grave, where she buried a small gold object. She had once given Jimmy a tiny cloth bear, which he always carried in his pocket, and he had it with him on his last raid. He had given her a little gold bear that she had kept through the past 64 years since his death. Now, she wanted it to be with him. As she stood, looking at the grave before leaving, she remembered that Jimmy's crew, Arthur Hardy and John Briggs, had been over for supper at "Rose Cottage" the night before the raid on August 28, 1941. They are buried beside him.

Bar died in 2008. Her ashes are buried in the Beechwood Cemetery in Ottawa next to Alastair Campbell. Some of her ashes are also buried with Jimmy in his grave.

Afterword 237

Jimmy's grave today in Crooswijk Cemetary, Rotterdam.

To Friends
James O. Alexander

Diverse flowers of many colors blooming through the day.
Their beauty is but momentary, it soon will fade away.
The straight majestic trees, that stand so tall and high
Their glory will not last; it soon will pass them by.

Oh! The beauty of the fields, as they stretch to meet the sky.
In the winter it will go, and the snow o'er them will lie.
And the music of the brooks, as they wind their sleepy path.
And the wonder of the fire, as it burns within the hearth.

The glory of the sun as in the far-off west
Crimson majesty doth glow, e're it leaves the world at rest.
These memories do not last, this beauty soon is gone.
But the beauty of our friends is ever living on.

Long after friends have left us, their memory still will last.
The memory of those happy days, those days that now are past.
And we will not forget them; until at last we be
With them once more united, for all eternity.

J.O. Alexander's
QUEBEC FAMILY TREE

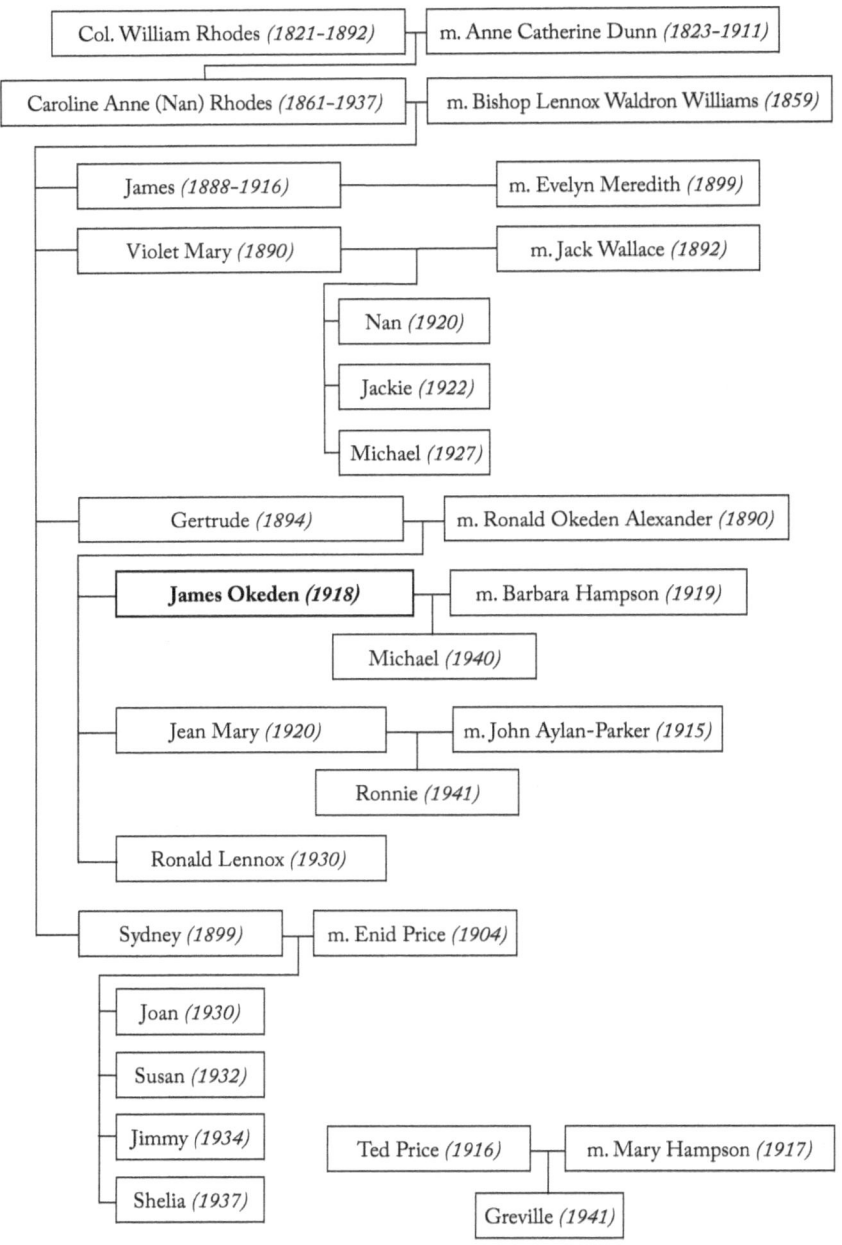

Col. William Rhodes *(1821-1892)* — m. Anne Catherine Dunn *(1823-1911)*

Caroline Anne (Nan) Rhodes *(1861-1937)* — m. Bishop Lennox Waldron Williams *(1859)*

- James *(1888-1916)* — m. Evelyn Meredith *(1899)*
- Violet Mary *(1890)* — m. Jack Wallace *(1892)*
  - Nan *(1920)*
  - Jackie *(1922)*
  - Michael *(1927)*
- Gertrude *(1894)* — m. Ronald Okeden Alexander *(1890)*
  - **James Okeden *(1918)*** — m. Barbara Hampson *(1919)*
    - Michael *(1940)*
  - Jean Mary *(1920)* — m. John Aylan-Parker *(1915)*
    - Ronnie *(1941)*
  - Ronald Lennox *(1930)*
- Sydney *(1899)* — m. Enid Price *(1904)*
  - Joan *(1930)*
  - Susan *(1932)*
  - Jimmy *(1934)*
  - Shelia *(1937)*

Ted Price *(1916)* — m. Mary Hampson *(1917)*
- Greville *(1941)*

J.O. Alexander's
BRITISH FAMILY TREE

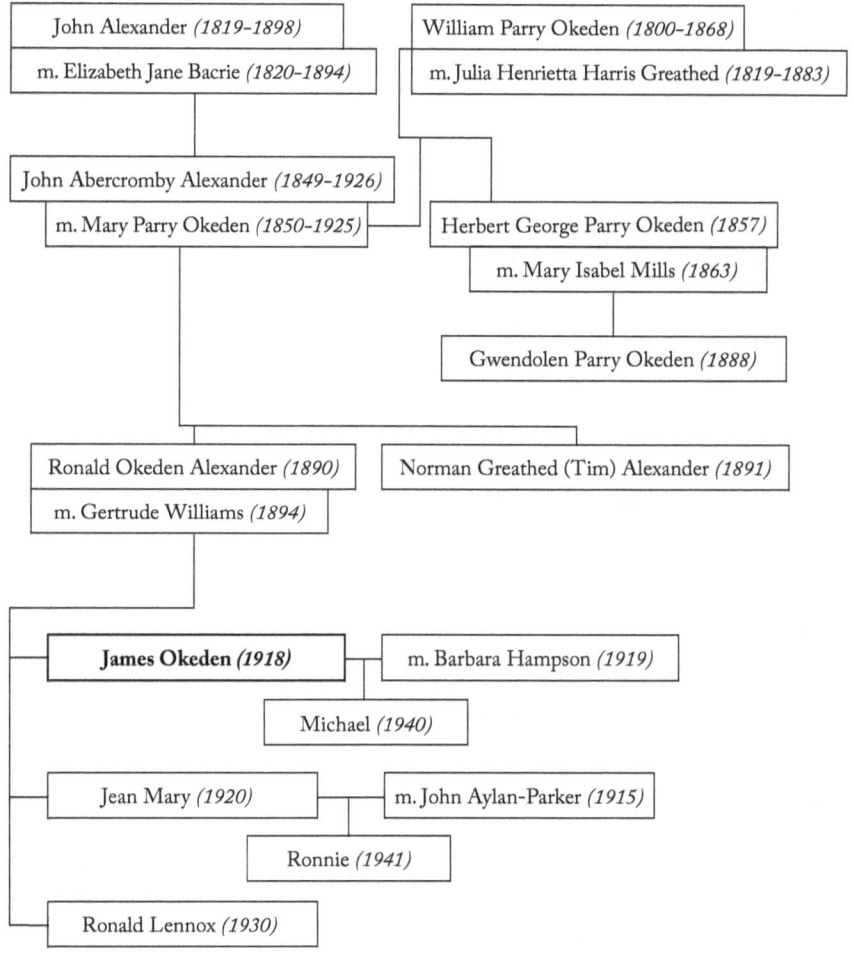

NOTES:

This is a partial family tree for J.O. Alexander's ancestors and relatives. Names and dates represent only those who were alive or died during the years 1918-1941.

Ted Price and Mary Hampson were related to J.O. Alexander through marriage. Ted was Enid Price's brother and Mary was Barbara Hampson's sister.

SOURCES

Most of this narrative was inspired and created from Jimmy's own letters, diaries, photographs and home movies. Because his letters seldom described the daily reports of the war, I had to look to other sources to provide the larger context in which his life took place during those years. Periodicals such as The Guardian, Daily Mirror, the Observer and the Daily Telegraph were the most helpful. Additionally, his father's memoirs which were published after his death, provided background and historical context, as well as stories of Jimmy's childhood. Other sources included books, many of which I have listed below.

I was surprised to discover so much written after the war by pilots who had flown Blenheims. Some of them describe the same bombing operations that Jimmy flew and even mentioned him by name. The August 28, 1941, raid on Rotterdam is detailed in several books and newspapers. I was able to obtain a photocopy of the logbook kept by John Briggs on the day they crashed. Somehow it was retrieved from the wreckage of Jimmy's plane and is now in safekeeping in the National Archives in London. The photograph of the remains of Jimmy's aircraft in Schiedam is courtesy of the Nederlands Institute voor Militaire Historie.

A Wing Commander. Bombers' Battle; Bomber Command's Three Years of War, by a Wing Commander. With a Foreword by Air Marshal Sir Arthur Harris, Riverside Press, Edinburgh, 1943, pp. 134, 135. (Description of Rotterdam raid, August 28, 1941)

Allport, Alan. *Britain at Bay.* The Epic Story of the Second World War, 1938-1941. Alfred A. Knopf, 2020.

Barton, Brian. *The Blitz.* The Blackstaff Press, 1989.

Bond, Geoffrey. *Lancastria.* Oldbourne Press, UK, 1959.

Bowman, Martin.W. *Daylight Bombing Operations 1939-1942.* 2014th ed., Pen and Sword, 2014, p. 75,84,85.

Bright, Stephen. *Z Force on the Ground, the Canadian deployment to Iceland*, 1940-41 Canadian Military History, Volume 31, Issue 1.

Falconer, Jonathan. *RAF Bomber Command Operations Manual.* Haynes Publishing UK, 2018.

Gibson, Guy. *Enemy Coast Ahead.* Goodall Publications, 1946, p. 166. (First-hand story of what it was like to be in Bomber Command and how the women, wives and girlfriends, played their part.)

Gillman, Ronald Edward. *The Shiphunters.* Cox & Wyman, 1976.

Harris, Arthur. *Bomber Offensive.* Pen and Sword, 2005.

Hastings, Max. *Bomber Command.* Zenith Press, 2013.

Hudson, Derek, and John Sweetman. *Bomber Crew.* Little Brown UK, 2005.

Lake, Jon. *Blenheim Squadrons of World War 2.* Osprey Publishing UK, 1998.

McPherson, James. *For Cause and Comrades.* Oxford University Press, 1997.

Onderwater, Hans. *En Toen Was Het Stil...*, Uitgeverij Hollandia, Netherlands 1981.

Panton, Alistair. *Six Weeks of Blenheim Summer.* Penguin, UK, 2018.

Passmore, Richard. *Blenheim Boy.* The Pitman Press UK, 1981.

Rivaz, RC. *Tail Gunner.* Jarrold's Publishers 1943.

Royal Military College of Canada Review, 1936-1939.

Terraine, John. *The Right of the Line.* Pen and Sword, 2010. (Royal Air Force History in World War II)

PHOTOGRAPH SOURCES:
p. 1 Source: Imperial War Museum
p.222 Source: The Illustrated London News, Sept 6, 1941
p.229 Source: Nederlands Instituut voor Militaire Historie

ACKNOWLEDGEMENTS

In writing this book I learned that while an author is alone in one sense, the task cannot be accomplished without the help and involvement of many others. This comes in a wide variety of forms. Had Jimmy's letters and diaries not been saved by his parents, his wife and several other relatives, his story would not have been told. Letters were the primary communication of news between people away from each other and served also as a record and a memory. I am truly grateful to Gertrude, Jimmy's mother, to Bar and to his aunts, Mary and Enid, for keeping his letters and for sending them to me. In the years before writing this book I had brief conversations about Jimmy with his sister Jean, his mother, his Aunt Mary (Wallace), Bar's friend Anne Byers, Ted Price and Gwen St. John at Stutton House. They gave me important glimpses of Jimmy's life.

It has taken me four years to complete this book during which my wife, Judy, never complained about my preoccupation with the story, what I was learning from my research and my insistence on talking about it. She was always there to encourage me and to read over parts of my drafts. Others in my family showed their interest and support: my son Jim after reading an early draft and my three grandsons, one of whom is in the Air Force, frequently asking when it would be finished and ready for them to read. All this helped to keep the project moving. When later drafts of the manuscript emerged, my readers: Alan Evans, Roger Lewis, Joan Ballantyne, Ian Blackwell and Lewis Evans asked useful questions and provided creative ideas and helpful suggestions and even corrections.

As the author, I learned that what I had prepared was simply the raw materials, and it was the editors who turned them into finished goods. I want to thank LeeLee Goodson for skillfully editing it into final form and Sally Stetson for her professional design of the cover and layout. They raised the level of excitement as we grew closer to the end. From the time I began writing, my daughter, Nan Doyal, was a helpful critic, offering ideas and continually making creative and constructive suggestions. These exchanges usually happened while we hiked together up Mount Mansfield in Vermont, with our Australian Shepherds. An author herself, she guided the effort through a sometimes stressful but hugely rewarding experience; and as its publisher and editor, she deserves great credit and thanks for bringing it all to maturity.

Ronald Alexander and his grandson Michael, Victoria, British Columbia 1942.

Michael Alexander was born in England, raised in Canada, and currently resides in the United States. He spent his early career in accounting, management consulting, strategic planning, and investment banking, including roles as International Executive Partner at Deloitte and Director of the Financial Accounting Standards Board (FASB).

In 1989, he merged his lifelong passion for history and culture with his business expertise and founded The International Forum – a global organization with a mission to connect business leaders from around the world by engaging them on current issues while integrating perspectives from science, society, art, history, technology, music, and culture.

In 2021, he began a focused effort to reconstruct his father's life story (James O. Alexander was a Royal Air Force bomber pilot, killed in World War II) and create a written record for his children and grandchildren. This endeavor evolved into a larger project—a discovery of a time and place that mirrored contemporary challenges and a legacy from which others could learn. *On The Wing of Eternity* is a first-person narrative of a young man's short but full life, compiled from journals, letters, and personal accounts.

Michael is a graduate of McGill University in Canada. He and his wife Judy, live in Boca Grande, Florida with their Australian Shepherd.

www.ingramcontent.com/pod-product-compliance
Lightning Source LLC
Chambersburg PA
CBHW020402080526
44584CB00014B/1135